INFUSED

INFUSED

ARLINDA MCGLOTHIN-MCKINLEY

PRINTED IN THE UNITED STATES OF AMERICA

Cover design by Arlinda Christine
Edited by Tenita Johnson with So It Is Written LLC

Dedication

To my mother & father
James E. McGlothin & Natalie M. McGlothin

Thanks for always believing that the storms would pass and instilling in me to thank God for it being as well as it is.

To God be the glory for the things He has done.

At this moment I realize how unimportant I am to you
Yet how important I am to me.
I matter even if you don't think so.

From *Ghetto Chick*
"At This Moment
©2009

Preface

In 2009 I self-published my first book, *Ghetto Chick*. *Ghetto Chick* is a book of poetry and writings based on my experiences from 2007 to 2009. During that time my husband had left me with two adorable sons and several months later, I met up with a poet from the bayou. In that relationship with the poet I began to write and dream of publishing my own books.

Well, here it is February 2019 and I have finally relaunched something special with *Infused*. *Infused* tells the story of the writings in Ghetto Chick. It's a love story of two people from different worlds that came together and tried to make love work.

I hope that you enjoy the story of Lindar and Cajun.

INFUSED

Not At Christmas

"Hey, Mary. What are you doing?"

"Hey, Lindar. What's up?"

"Can we do lunch? Like now!"

"You okay?"

"No. Need to get out. Meet me at Cooker's."

"Now! I…"

"Mary, look…he went home."

"What! It's Christmastime."

Lindar replayed the scene over and over again. She had been shopping for Christmas Day. Cajun had been pacing the house all day. He must've found the perfect gift for her, which he didn't want her to know about. This was their second Christmas together, so he knew her pretty well by now.

She had prepared a wonderful meal for their first *real* Christmas together. Last year, they were just friends. But soon, they would be married. Lindar had settled in, doing all the preparations that she did not get to experience with Tito. The excitement overcame her whenever she thought of his reaction to the engraved Movado watch she had purchased as his gift. TJ was on a date, and Lindar agreed to pick them up from the movies.

Upon returning home, Lindar had an uneasy feeling. A still emptiness met her at the door. On the microwave was a note that read, "I'm going home for Christmas."

Not Christmas! What about me, the boys, dinner? Damn, the watch.

She thought about calling or texting Cajun. Realizing that her version of Christmas was ruined, she glazed the ham, set the oven timer and turned on The Word Network. *Where is Pastor Jamal Bryant when you need him?*

"Thanks, Mary."

"Don't worry about it. I needed a timeout."

"Hello, ladies. What can I get for you?" The waiter asked.

"I would like two Amaretto Sours. I'll take one now and as soon as you think that I am almost finished, bring me the next one."

"Lindar! What the hell is wrong with you?"

"Oh! I'll also take the chicken and cheese with loaded mashed potatoes. And where are those biscuits? Mary, please order. It's on me."

"I need a minute, sir," Mary responded. Lindar, did you drive? You don't drink often."

"You know what? I don't drink often, but I need to drink right now. Where is he?"

"Who?"

"Our server."

Mary knew Lindar had been having a hard time lately. Her divorce was final, and she was seeing a guy whom she was somewhat unsure of. She had no idea Lindar was this bad off.

The server returned with their drinks and, in two gulps, Lindar's drink was gone.

"Mary, I think I need a vacation. Let's go somewhere."

"Lord, what is wrong with my friend?"

"We can take the kids and our dog, Nia. I have a timeshare in South America. Come on! I need to get away." Lindar laughed uncontrollably.

"Nia can't go to South America? I better Google that."

Mary got a serious look on her face and looked her dear friend in her eyes.

"What about him? What about Cajun?"

Lindar sighed as she toyed with her orange slice attached to her empty glass.

"What *about* him? I don't think I really care anymore. A new year is coming. I need to do a new thing."

"Speaking of a new thing, when are you coming back to church? Have you read your Bible today? You need to pray about this."

"I have been praying. I just don't know why Cajun has me so messed up over him. Or is it me? Spencer keeps telling me my self-esteem is low. She tells me that he is just using me for my hot water."

Both women laughed uncontrollably, imagining Spencer giving out her 18-year-old thoughts of the day.

"Lindar! Hot water?"

"Yes, Mary. That girl has so much to grow through. She is on her road to understanding. Bless her heart."

After finishing drinks and lunch, Mary and Lindar made their way to the car. Both women were silent, but it spoke volumes to Lindar's situation.

"You know what? I have some decisions to make. I know this is not God's best for me. I have to get it together."

"Girl, God knows your heart. You have to stay in prayer."

"I know," Lindar said, as she reached for her car door.

"But I also feel bad for Cajun. You know God has His hands on you. The Bible says touch not my anointed and…"

"Do my servant no harm."

"Yeah, I just hope he is ready for the repercussions of what he is doing to you. He isn't just breaking your heart. He is crushing it."

Nueve

Skipped heartbeats, staring eyes, when your presence is clear.
The day of our first encounter had to be spring, had to be summer.

The air warm, sun shining. It had to be spring, had to be summer.
Voice so rich and melodic, beckoning me from existence.

Our eyes and spirits magnetized to each other, transcending years
past and future.

In that present, we could not see that we were bonded for eternity
before eternity.

Time slips past and, still, we cannot determine our fate, our reason.
We discover temporary bliss and spirits, unlike the ones we possess.
Journeys unnecessarily taken, hearts unnecessarily broken.
Continuing on, we seek each other in others.
Formulating ideas of ideal, the pain is unreal.

Fall comes and goes, and our spirits meet up again.
More like a collision of hearts not expecting, not realizing that those
hearts belong to each other.

Winter turns into spring. Daily, our paths cross in amazement of
each other.
Open eyes meet in the dark, caresses important, kisses undenied.
Submission required.

Waiting for this moment never dreamed of is worth more than any
moment ever dreamed of.

Skipped heartbeats, staring eyes, when your presence is clear.
The day of our first encounter had to be spring, had to be summer.

The day I met him, I was working in my basement office when I heard his voice. I had to leave my desk and see who he was. I was intrigued and I had to introduce myself.

"Hi. My name is Lindar."

Lindar extended her hand to his.

"Hello. My name is Cajun. Nice to meet chu. Do chu work 'ere?"

"Yes, this is my office." Lindar turned to an open door.

"Awright. I have to check you out then."

"I look forward to it."

That was the defining moment of rising publisher, Lindar, and the incredible poet, Cajun. Neither knew at that time that almost a decade later, they would be in a relationship, full of twists and deception.

Thinking back on that day, I probably should have stayed in my office and spoke to him in passing. *How could he be so cruel, so heartless? Why do I attract selfish men? Is there a subliminal signal that I give off? All selfish MFs come to me and treat me like dirt!*

First, my son's father. Now *this*. Cajun was supposed to be different. This relationship started off so unexpectedly. And that's just how it seemed to be ending – *unexpectedly.*

Damn It, Spencer

"Auntie, I believe that your self-esteem is low and that your self-confidence is shot. I've never seen you like this over a man. Do you hear what he says to you? Do you read the texts? He told you to die in your sleep, and that you were dumb and stupid. Come on, now. What do you see in him? He needs to leave you alone. Tell him to go."

Lindar couldn't take anymore of Spencer's bantering.

"Okay! Okay! Spencer, I hear you!"

"No, I don't think you do. I believe Cajun has a hold on you. Ain't he from Louisiana? Have you seen *Eve's Bayou*? Maybe we should watch that …. and that other movie."

Lindar prayed silently, *Lord, give me the strength to not cuss my niece out! She is working on my negative nerves. I know she means well, but goodness gracious! Does she ever stop?*

"Do your hear me, Lindar? The movie about the serpent and…and…and…"

"The rainbow, Spencer! *The Serpent and the Rainbow*!"

"Okay! We need to watch those movies. Maybe we can figure out why he treats you so bad. But then, we need a movie to see why you allow him to treat you the way he does. We need a Terry McMillan movie for that."

As if she had come up with the perfect thought, she chimed in, "I know, Lindar! We can watch *Disappearing Acts*. The one with Sanaa Lathan and somebody."

"You have had one boyfriend since 7th grade. You are only 18. You have no idea about loving a man."

"Oh! Is *that* what this is? You loving a man that calls you names and treats you bad."

"It ain't that bad. He has a good heart, and he is compassionate and kind, at times."

"At times? It don't weigh right. The good should outweigh the bad."

"You know it wasn't like this in the beginning. I don't know what happened. I remember sitting around, watching movies by candlelight. Talking about poetry and my future company, Lindar Publishing. Then, it was cool. He don't even write anymore. The streets are his woman now. He's so creative, so loving, so…"

"He's so a loser. Auntie, you could do better than him. You have degrees, family and friends that love you, and your company is getting more and more popular. Oprah and Tyra will be calling you soon."

"But so much of the creativity of Lindar Publishing is driven by Cajun's push for me to be at my best when I write. *Ghetto Chick* wouldn't even exist without him."

"Yeah, sure. *Ghetto Chick* is about your experiences with men."

"Cajun inspired that. I can't deny that."

"You give him too much credit. You are a talented writer. People love what you have to say. You have a lot to say to the world. Cajun is holding you back from all of that."

"Sometimes I miss talking to him."

"What? Him calling you a fat ass bitch, or dumb and stupid?"

"Damn it, Spencer!

Thanksgiving

It was around Thanksgiving when I noticed a strange phone number appear on my caller I.D. I had decided it was Tito, and God knows we had nothing to talk about. So, the phone simply rang and rang. Tito needed to figure out what he wanted. Crack, or our boys and me? Right now, crack was the undisputed champion.

Birthdays are so important to me. This year, Mia, Mary and I dined on shrimp and Dom Pérignon. We had a ball. There was food, our children and laughter. On that night, the phone rang again.

"Hello."

"How are you doing, Lindar?"

This can't be who I think it is. I haven't heard from him since Katrina. What in the world?

"Love, you don't know who this is?"

"Hi, Cajun. How have you been?"

I met Cajun in the late 90s. He was always a weakness for me. We spoke every odd year. Sounds strange, but it is true. Sure enough, it was an odd year: 2007.

"I've been better. How about you?"

"Good, real good. Look, I am celebrating my birthday; can I call you later?"

"A'ight. I'll be here."

"Well, it may not be tonight."

"And I'll still be here waiting for you to call."

Hmm! Lindar wondered. *What will I learn from this? Cajun and I, for one reason or another, don't last long.*

By midnight, the candles were blown out and everyone was ready to leave.

"Mia and Mary, thanks for celebrating my day with me. What a year this has been! I'm so glad to have friends like you."

"Lindar, I love you, too. Now I got to make it home without getting stopped by a DUI checkpoint."

"Mary, please don't have Bill hunting me down."

The women laughed as they walked to the door. Lindar surveyed the room. Cleaning wasn't required because Mia was so meticulous. Tito Jr. (TJ) and Benji were passed out in their rooms. Those boys made Lindar want to breathe daily. TJ was becoming a teenager. He was so handsome and gracious. Of everyone in the family, he had suffered the most in dealing with his father's addiction. Benji was almost the spitting image of his older brother. The love they had for one another was amazing. Benji has a humorous side to him that kept everyone laughing all the time.

Lindar wanted the absolute best for them. That was the main reason why she set out to create Lindar Publishing. She knew she had a gift in writing. She knew she had something to say and that it could bring in a serious income into her household. Lindar had married Tito three years ago. It seemed as if it was over before it started. Living with an addict is something that can only be explained by someone with a similar experience. Sometimes, Lindar didn't know if Tito had tried hard enough to not use. Since they'd been married, he had been to two different rehab facilities. Just when it seemed that the family was on the road to something positive, Tito made his own decision.

It had been ten months since Tito left his family. Lindar had adjusted to the strained finances and lonely nights. Her thoughts of reconciliation failed with each day of not seeing or hearing from her husband. The hardest part for her had been that she believed she had failed God by thinking about divorce—though she felt it was no sense in being married and alone, raising the boys.

❧

"Hi, Cajun!"

"Why do chu always say my name? I hate when people say it."

"I like your name. It's different. I don't know anyone with a name like yours. So whenever I have a chance to say it I do. Cajun, Cajun, Cajun.

Both Lindar and Cajun smiled at the thought of being back in touch. Cajun always knew Lindar would be there for him, even though they did not stay in touch often. At this moment, he needed her friendship more than ever.

"A'ight. Wit chu been up to? How's Tito?"

"He is fine. Me, just going to school, teaching and taking care of the boys."

"Hold up, now. Slow it down. Teaching? Boys?"

"Yeah, I teach English and, after I got married, I had Benji."

Cajun knew a little about Lindar's marriage. He had tried to warn her that maybe she should rethink that decision.

"Married? Huh?"

"Yeah, it didn't last though. He left. But other than that, I'm okay."

"Remember when I called chu 'bout that?"

"Cajun, that was after Katrina. I was already married, already pregnant. Anyway, how are you?"

"Man, I don't even want to go into it. But I do have a daughter here in the city."

"Oh! You seeing someone?"

"Naw, I just got a daughter that lives in the city."

"What is her name?"

"Helena."

"That's pretty."

"I named her. Wat chu going to do about yur husband?"

"I don't know. I want to get a divorce, but it's about money and timing. Right now, I just don't think about it."

14

Since Tito had left, Lindar haven't had many conversations with men. Yet, here she sat for over an hour talking non-stop.

"Hey, Cajun. I need to go. Thanks for calling. Take care."

"Take care?"

"You know how we do? We talk every so often and catch up. We've caught up. You have a daughter and sound well. I am a teacher. I have a new son and I am getting a divorce. We're caught up. I have to go."

"Can I call chu again?"

"For what?"

"Look, I just need someone to talk to."

"Whatever. I don't care."

Cajun sighed. "I'll call chu. A'ight?"

"Bye."

Lindar couldn't imagine what he would want to talk about. They had stayed in touch, but not to the extent of talking daily. Well, he did say he needed someone to talk to.

Fit Me In

"I have to go, Cajun. You'll have me on the phone all night. I have to get up early for work."

"Look, I'll talk to you when chu get off werk."

"We can't talk all the time. We don't have a reason to for real."

"Is that how I get handled?"

"What?" Lindar laughed at Cajun's usual use of words.

"Nothing. Chu haven't laughed like this in a minute, have you?"

"True, but we have lives to lead. We spend way too much time talking and texting. I am a mother and I have responsibilities."

"So, chu ain't gonna call?"

"I will call you, but not often."

That last statement proved to be a lie. As soon as Lindar was off work, she and Cajun were on the phone like teenagers with a high school crush. When she wasn't talking to him, she was taking care of her home and the boys. But once home was settled, and the boys were in the bed asleep, they would continue wherever they left off and talk for hours.

They discussed their children and failed relationships. Each shared their wounded stories, not knowing that they were in the process of creating

another heartache. Lindar looked forward to Cajun's calls and was trying to find balance between Cajun and the rest of her life. Basketball season would start up soon. Lindar knew that took priority in TJ's life and that Cajun would have to take a back seat.

It was a dismal Sunday afternoon in December when Lindar returned from church. She was making every effort to clean the kitchen, which was full of pots and pans, her least favorite to clean. Benji was wandering around the house, competing for Mommy's attention.

Cajun called Lindar as soon as she reached home.

"Boy, I can't clean and talk to you. I have to call you later."

"I'll do it for chu," Cajun replied.

"Do what?"

"Whadever you're trying to do."

"I am scrubbing pots and pans!" Lindar exclaimed.

"So! I'll be there. Where you live?"

"Cajun?"

"Come on, darlin'. Where you stay?"

"I can't explain it without you getting lost."

"Try me."

"For real?"

Within 20 minutes, Cajun was standing at her front door.

"Hey!"

"Hey, Cajun!"

"Can I come in?"

Lindar moved out of the doorway and allowed Cajun to enter her home—and, subsequently, her life.

"You don't have to clean my kitchen."

Cajun walked past Lindar and proceeded to clean the sink full of pots and pans.

"If I say I'm going to do something, I'm gonna do it. Tito here?"

"No, he's at practice. This is my son, Benji."

Benji hid behind his mother's legs and pierced his eyes at Cajun.

Cajun walked closer and extended his hand to Benji.

"How chu doing?"

Benji did not move.

"He doesn't take to strangers well," Lindar said apologetically. "Sorry. Benji, say hello." Benji grabbed his mother's pants legs tighter.

"We'll sit in the living room. Let me know if you need something."

"I need a sponge," Cajun responded.

Lindar walked into the kitchen and opened the cabinet under the sink, pulling out a yellow sponge. She didn't realize that he'd watched her every move. As she handed Cajun the sponge, she felt an undeniable energy. It was as if they were in sync with each other's actions. Cajun took the sponge from Lindar and noticed something about her that he'd never paid much attention to. He was attracted to her. With that knowledge now validated, he continued cleaning her kitchen.

Benji had fallen asleep on Lindar as they watched *Little Bill* on the chaise lounge. She wanted to put him in a bed, but she was tired herself. Cajun walked into the room as Lindar debated where to move her body so that she wouldn't wake Benji.

"Where do you want Benji?"

"In my room."

Without question, Cajun lifted Benji off Lindar and put him on Lindar's bed. After covering Benji, he came back in the living room and sat across from Lindar.

"Thanks, Cajun. I truly appreciate that."

"No problem."

"So, do you always clean people's kitchens?"

"Naw!"

"Are you hungry?"

"No, I'm cool, Lindar. We cool chillin' like this."

Lindar and Cajun spent the remainder of the evening watching TV and talking. TJ had come in from practice and went straight to bed. The boys were sleeping peacefully and Lindar was in the company of her male friend. She could not remember her home being so peaceful. The weird part was that it felt normal.

Lindar's phone rang and Mia's name blinked across the screen.

"Mia!"

"Lindar, we are on our way over."

"You and Spencer? Coming over now?"

"Yeah, I finished dinner and we have to run to the store. So we are stopping by."

"I have company."

"Who? Tito?"

"No. Cajun."

"Cajun?"

"Yeah, he came over after church."

"Bye!"

Lindar knew, "Bye!" meant, "We'll be there in less than ten." She wondered what Spencer would think.

"Hey, Mia. Hey, Spencer. I have someone I want you to meet. This is Cajun," Lindar said. Cajun stood up and shook hands with Mia and Spencer.

"Nice to meet y'all."

"I am Lindar's friend, Mia. I remember you from years ago. This is my daughter, Spencer."

❧

Lindar and Mia had been friends since junior high school. Now grown up, they attended church together and often got together on Sunday afternoons to just hang out. They were more like sisters than friends. Spencer was in her senior year of high school and getting ready for all that senior year had to offer. Spencer was often very opinionated when it came to Lindar's and Mia's relationship issues. She never understood why they settled for nonsense. She vowed that she would never deal with situations that her mother and aunt had.

Spencer sat across from Lindar and Cajun, and stared at her aunt. She had never seen her aunt with anyone other than Tito. So, this was new for her to see Lindar with a man—a man whom she didn't know anything about.

When it seemed to be the right thing to do, Cajun prepared to go home. He had a visit with his daughter the next day, and he needed to be prepared for Helena's year-old energy.

"Lindar, I want to get something for my daughter. Would chu' go with me to pick something out?"

"Sure. Let me get my coat and tell Mia that I will be right back."

"A'ight."

That night on the phone, the conversation between Lindar and Cajun was a little different than their previous conversations.

"How was yur day?" Cajun asked.

"It was good. Thank you. And yours?"

"Good. Thanks for helping me pick out a toy. Sometimes I just don't know what to get for her."

"Not a problem."

"Let me ask chu a question."

"Go ahead," Lindar beckoned.

"Yur marriage, is it really over?"

"Pretty much. He left in January and I have not heard from him since then."

"Do you date?"

"I went on a date a couple of weeks ago. I am not putting myself out there for real. Why?"

"Just asking."

"Do *you* date?" Lindar countered.

"Love, all I want is my daughter."

"I hear you."

Hoop Dreams

TJ had been playing basketball since third grade. Now he was starting varsity his freshman year of high school. Lindar was so proud of him. Basketball season was filled with study tables, practices, games and fast-food restaurants. Tonight was a home game against Amelia. TJ's school was not known for having a good basketball team. But, as a parent, all Lindar could do was go to the games and cheer the team on.

"Auntie, you got money for snacks?"

"Taylor, do you ever bring money to the games?"

"Why, when you and Nana are here?"

Lindar reached in her purse and gave Taylor $5.

"Now take Benji with you. God knows if you come back here with a snack and don't have one for him, he will have a fit."

"True."

"True? Don't you attend the best high school in the city? Is that all you can say is true?"

"Yep!"

"Lord help us."

TJ generally had a nice crowd of friends and family attending his games, and tonight was no different. It was a time to not only watch TJ play, but to catch up on everyone's week. Lindar felt her phone constantly going off. She couldn't imagine who would be interrupting basketball time. She looked at her phone and saw that Cajun had texted and called her several times. She texted him back.

Hey, Cajun. I am at TJ's game. What's up?

Fit me in.

Fit you in where? I don't understand.

I want to see you this weekend.

Cajun we just got back in touch. We don't know each other like that.

Lindar, I want to spend time with you and your sons.

Lindar could not believe what she was hearing. She had to think about what he was asking. She didn't let just anyone come into her world. Though she had always adored Cajun, she was unsure of his intentions.

Cajun, let me think it over. I'll let you know. Okay?

Okay.

I will text you or call you after the game is over.

How is he playing?

He is doing okay. I gotta go.

A'ight.

"Mia, Cajun just asked to see me this weekend."

"What? What are you going to do?"

"I don't know. We had a nice time last Sunday and, earlier this week when Nia got sick and threw up several times, Cajun came over and cleaned her up."

"Did he spend the night?"

"Yeah...he..."

"Shut up! Lindar!"

"No! No! We slept on the floor while watching TV."

"Whatever. You didn't tell me about that."

23

"There was nothing to tell."

"Well, it might be something to tell this weekend."

"I don't know. I have to talk it over with TJ. His thoughts count, too. They have been through a lot, and bringing another "friend" into the picture? I don't know."

"Lindar, you are good to include your sons in your decisions. You know you have to move on, too. Tito has been gone since January, and it don't look like he's coming back."

"I just want everyone to be comfortable."

"How comfortable do you want Cajun to be?" Mia said with a smirk.

"Girl, please!" Lindar responded, blushing.

❦

"Good game, TJ. How do you feel?"

"Tired and hungry."

"Where do you want to eat?"

"The usual, Mom. I am whooped. They was trying to kill me."

"Yeah, I saw that. Benji is already sleep. I'll get him something anyway. Can I ask you a question?"

"Shoot."

"How do you feel about Cajun coming to visit more often?"

"I don't care. He ain't going to be cussing all the time, is he?"

"Why is that all that you remember about him?" Lindar and TJ laughed because he was telling the truth. When TJ was younger, and he was around Cajun, the only thing TJ could remember was Cajun's use of profanity.

"I don't know. It has always stayed with me. It should be cool though, Ma. He seems cool."

⤸

"Cajun, if you still want to visit this weekend, you can."

"How about tonight?"

"How about no!" Lindar exclaimed.

"Lindar, please? I want to see you. I have thought about chu all day."

"Whatever, Cajun!"

"We can just watch a movie and talk. That's all."

"That's all?"

"Yea'."

"Well, I have to stop at Mickey D's. I should be home in about an hour or so."

"Cool. I'll be ova' about ten."

Lindar sat on the phone in silence.

"Lindar?"

"Yes?"

"Ten?" Cajun asked.

"Whatever. I gotta go."

⤸

Benji was pretty much sleep for the night and TJ soon followed behind him. The atmosphere was different. With lights out, sounds of the TV filled the room. Lindar tried to set aside the kiss they shared during the week. She was not prepared for his intensity or his passion. Had she not been sitting down, she probably would have needed to. Now they were alone again.

"Cajun, I have a movie we could watch. It's called *Something New* with Sanaa Lathan."

"What channel?"

"It's On Demand. Do you want to watch it?"

"Sure."

Lindar took the remote and found *Something New* on the On Demand Channel. She sat in her favorite place in the living room.

"This don't seem like your kind of movie. You seem like an action- packed, get-the-drug-dealer movie watcher."

"You would be surprised. Can I sit with you?" Cajun asked.

"Sure."

Lindar moved so that Cajun could sit next to her on the chaise lounge. Now her mind was really messed up.

Staying up late with Cajun watching a movie, while he sits next to me. If only my marriage had worked, I would not have to do this damn dating thing, she thought. Slowly, she became comfortable and soon, she fell asleep in Cajun's arms. She awoke a while later, surprised that the movie was still on.

"I thought you would have changed the channel," Lindar said.

"Naw, I liked it. I even called my sister and told her about it."

"Well, I am going to bed. I have to go to the grocery store in the morning. Are you staying?"

"Yea'. I'll go with chu," Cajun responded.

"You don't have to. I am used to going early on Saturday mornings."

"Lindar, let me go with you. Stop telling me no."

As their eyes met, Lindar came to the reality that Cajun was trying to be more than her friend. She didn't know how to deal with that.

"We'll see."

"I'll be up."

"Good night, Cajun."

"Good night, luv."

Lindar got up from the chaise lounge and went into her room, where she prepared herself for much needed sleep. She laid there and watched the moonlight spill from the bay windows. She wondered what was going to happen between Cajun and her. Just as she was about to go to sleep, she received a text.

You okay?

Yeah, I am fine.

You want me to get you some water or something?

I will get it when I take the dog out.

I got you.

Within in a minute, Cajun brought Lindar some water and kissed her good night. Afterwards, he proceeded to let Nia out. Once he was back in, Lindar remotely set the house alarm system. She sat up and thought, *He has not denied one thing I've asked of him yet. Maybe I will see what he is about. Maybe.*

He Never Denies Me

It can be the most amazing feeling when you meet a person who fulfills your wishes, your wants and your needs. You see it on television and you read about it. But oftentimes, it seems like an illusion.

"That will never happen."

"It doesn't happen to me or my friends."

But, when it does happen, it's too good to be true.

He's no pushover. Push the wrong button and you could be in for a long day. He's southern. He's sweet. He's spiritual. His soul is beautiful. He was brought to earth to make me feel, drive me to create.

Water at midnight? His response is, "Do you want ice, too?" I fall asleep watching TV, I awake under a blanket. The dog is irritating everyone.

"I'll take him out."

"You for real?" I asked him. This can't be real. Let me see!

"I am hungry."

"What you want me to cook?"

"I have to go out for a minute."

"Wait, I'll drive."

Wow!

I can now say that I know what it feels like. He never denies me. It can be simple or complex, but he always says, "Yes." Sometimes, I ask just to hear his response to something that I don't need or want. He told me that he would do whatever I asked of him. I had to put him to the test.

Did he pass? Yes! So, I ask often. Even when he is tired and preoccupied, he never denies me.

Saturday

Lindar loved the mornings. She would often get up and go straight to the front of the house to view the different designs the sunlight drew on the walls throughout her open living room area. It was one of the many things she loved about her open space. Watching the sunlight fill up the open spaces always gave a serene feeling to her home. Mornings were special to Lindar. While the boys slept, she would get up and begin her morning tasks, including opening the venetian blinds, warming up a cup of lavender tea, and simply enjoying the silence of the morning.

Lindar had also learned that being one of the first people at the grocery store was like heaven on earth on Saturday mornings. No crowds to navigate through and no long wait at the checkout counter. She relished in the crispness of the morning air as she went to and from the store each Saturday. As she grabbed her seasonal parka and prepared to leave, she remembered Cajun's offer. But she pushed it out of her mind. He was probably still sleep, and she was used to going to the store alone. Hoping she had not bothered anyone's sleep, Lindar was stopped in her tracks as she saw Cajun putting on his jacket.

He had heard Lindar when she got up. He was going to make true on his promise to go with her. For some reason, he wanted to spend as much time with her as possible. There was something undeniable about her that drew him to her and her to him.

"Mornin', Luv! Let's go."

With that, Lindar and Cajun prepared to go Krogering. Before she left, she stopped by TJ's room and let him know she was leaving. She knew it was best to not check on her baby boy, Benji, because once he would begin to cry, Lindar would feel guilty about leaving him at home.

"TJ. I'll be back in about an hour."

"Okay, Mommy."

"You want something?"

"Waffles, pizza, orange juice, pizza rolls, milk…"

"Never mind. Just get up and go take care of your brother."

"Okay, Mama."

"Silly person. I'll call you when I get back."

Stepping outside, she could sense that winter was arriving soon. The early morning wind had a crispness that signaled colder nights and shorter days. Thanksgiving had passed and Christmas was near.

Nothing like dating in between seasons. Right after the turkey and right before the gift. Lindar wondered. *Is Cajun the turkey or the gift?*

"Wa chu thinkin'?"

"Nothing."

"Righ…" Cajun smiled as he looked over at Lindar.

"So, are you going in the store, too?"

"Sure am. Too cold to wait in the car."

"Okay," Lindar responded.

"Okay? Ummm. Plus I want to see how you shop. What a woman buys says a lot about her," Cajun retorted.

"So you eavesdropping on my grocery list, Cajun?"

"Yep, I need to see what I'm working with."

"Boy, please!"

"Boy? Is that how I get handled, Lindar?"

"How you get *handled*?"

The drive to the store was short. As they approached an open parking space, Cajun grabbed Lindar's hand, forcing her to stop talking.

"Yeah. Is that how I get handled? You know what? Imma teach chu' what I know. Then, you can handle it."

"Really now? You on some fly, slick stuff with me? You'd better watch out now. I can handle it *and you*."

Cajun smiled as he looked at Lindar with his eyes twinkling in the early morning sun. He knew she was intelligent and attractive, and a good mom. Now, he was seeing a new side of her. A side that could step to him. She could go word for word with him, without missing a breath. She didn't hide her naiveté, nor did she hide that, deep inside of her, there existed a portion of her that was *just like him*.

෨

This particular Saturday was cold and sunny. By afternoon, TJ had left for practice, and Benjamin was watching a series of *Caillou* and *Little Bill*. Lindar was writing out her lesson plans for the upcoming week. Creativity and structure drove her classroom lessons. She knew that if she missed a beat with her students, the day could turn out to be disastrous.

"What chu' up to?"

"Writing out plans for the week. Getting ready for Monday."

"Chu' know, writing is what you were born to do, Lindar?"

Lindar stopped working and gazed into Cajun's eyes, almost as if she wanted to find the answer for herself without him telling her.

"Really?"

"Yeah! Really."

"Hmmm…"

"Hmmm, what?"

"I've known you for years, but I have never shared anything with you about my desire to write," Lindar confided.

"'Cause I know err thing about chu'. Even the stuff chu' refuse to see."

"Stuff like what?"

"You sure chu' want to hear?" Cajun asked.

"Go."

"Writin', music, shy, scared. You hide behind your sons."

"Whatever, Cajun. You have no idea. You don't know me."

"What's the matter? Chu' mad, jealous or angry? And don't let nobody mention those boys! Do you sing, Lindar?"

"No!"

"Because you scared. You been hurt that bad that you don't use what's inside you."

Getting a little bothered by the direction of the conversation, Lindar decided to start dinner, hoping that Cajun would let the discussion die down … or just go away.

"Wha' chu' running from me? If you scared, say you scared!"

"Cajun, I think I'm gonna start dinner."

"No, no. Lemme. You sit here so I can help you see yourself."

"I don't need to see myself," Lindar responded.

"See, that's problem number one. Just for the record, chu' getting mad at me don't bother me."

"So, you gonna cook dinner?"

"Righ! Righ!"

"And I'm supposed to sit here and listen to you? No, no, sit here and see myself?"

"Little butterfly, I think chu' get it," Cajun said.

"Well, I'd rather go watch *Little Bill* than to sit here and…"

"And wha'? Listen to some truth about you. I tell you what. Gone in there and watch TV with Benji. This can wait til later."

Back in the living room, Lindar cuddled up with Benji as they shared in the familiar moment of watching a *Little Bill* episode. Benji loved this show and, the more Lindar watched, she could see the similarities in *Little Bill* and her own son. So inquisitive and outgoing. She knew that Benji would someday go on to do great things in life.

Cajun had cooked dinner, and Lindar and Benji were pleased as Cajun brought them plates of food to eat as they watched TV. The three of them sat around, eating and talking, almost like the family Lindar had envisioned when she married Tito. Over ten months had passed, and he had yet to even pick up the phone and attempt reconciliation. Now she and Cajun were steadily easing into this situation that would turn their already fragile friendship into love and disaster.

$$\approx$$

"So now that I have your attention, I want a favor."

"Cajun, what is it now?"

"Hold on, now. Don't get mad because I know more than you're willing to tell."

"So, what do you want from me?"

"Help me create a book of poetry?"

"Who?" Lindar asked.

"You? Luv, you gotta couple good books in chu'. Help me with mine." Cajun responded.

"I've never written a book. I don't even know where to start."

"Chu' never written a book yet. Stay right here."

Cajun went to the living room and brought Lindar a notebook filled with poetry.

"And this is?"

"My book. *My Unorganized Tablet*."

"Tablet?"

"Yea'. That's the name of my book," Cajun said.

Flicker

After dinner, Lindar put Benjamin in the bed. She always looked at him until he fell asleep. He was so handsome, so funny and so smart. She said a silent prayer over his life and kissed his chocolate cheek before turning the lights out.

TJ was with Coach White and, in the words of the youth, "That was a wrap." So, in the house on this cool autumn night, Cajun and Lindar sat with Cajun's notebook of unedited poetry. As Lindar sifted through each poem, she thanked God for her ability of understanding what he was trying to say. Lindar had worked with students with specific learning disabilities for years. One part of her job seemed to always entail figuring out what her students wanted to say in their writing. This was truly no different.

Through all of the spelling and grammatical errors, Lindar could see Cajun had an incredible talent for spoken word. For really tough poems, Cajun would read them and Lindar would edit them as he spoke. The night grew and grew into this surreal moment, as if it was right out of a movie. Cajun watched Lindar bring his tablet to life. As she worked into the night, he lit candles and incense, which seemed to provide a more creative mood. He grabbed another notebook and began working on new pieces.

It wasn't until she took a break that she gave attention to the ambiance that he had created. Looking over at Cajun, she saw him deep in thought. By the flicker of the candlelight, she sensed herself being drawn to him in ways she before didn't think were possible. Cajun was engrossed in his craft, but he could feel the warmth of Lindar's eyes on him.

"Cajun, for what you want, I can have it done by tomorrow evening."

"For what I really want, what can I have done by tonight?"

"Not a thin—"

Cajun moved toward Lindar the way a man does when he knows what he wants. Before Lindar could object, reject or push away, she was captured by his passion, and it engulfed her. She didn't think of her failed marriage or all of the lonely nights since January. All that mattered was right now, with Cajun showering her with the attention and affection she desired to have.

By Sunday morning, Lindar and Cajun were a couple— though neither one of them realized it. There was no way to control what was happening. They both needed solid ground to stand on and, for both of them, it simply felt good. While they were in this world, in this moment, neither would bring forth a much-needed conversation about the other people they were both detached from and attached to. Instead, they relished in the fact that, after months of hell, two friends had become lovers.

❧

The day had come and gone. The boys were in the bed, and so was Lindar. Cajun had left earlier in the evening after they had dinner with Lindar's friend, Mary. Cajun had a draft of his book and he was one happy man. With the TV on and a cup of tea in hand, Lindar reflected over her weekend with the brother from the Bayou. The signal from her wireless phone notified her of a text. She lifted her phone and pressed the show button. It was a message from Cajun.

He was a fool to leave chu' and the boys. I'm 'ere now. I got you, Luv.

Staring at the message, Lindar's mind went back to that day her husband left. She thought she would never want another man, or that another man would want her. Now Cajun had shown her that desire was still in her heart. She texted him back.

I'm glad you're here, but do me a favor. Please always be honest with me?

Darlin', chu got that from me. Chu' sumthing special. Holla at me tomorrow. Cajun texted back.

This Christmas

One perk of being a teacher was definitely Christmas break. This particular break was filled with love and basketball. Lindar, Cajun and Benjamin were at all of TJ's high school games. Afterwards, they would grab dinner or come home, and Lindar or Cajun would put a quick meal together.

Hesitation came from both ends. But, after celebrating Cajun's birthday, and their previous weekend together, whatever was developing between them flowed naturally into the Christmas break. By now, everyone in the home was getting into a familiar habit. Everyone was unknowingly filling in the gaps for what was seemingly missing in their lives. Cajun had the family life he had always desired to have. The boys had a male figure to go to in the house, and Lindar was able to put away her Superwoman cape and allow someone to help take care of her and the family's day-to-day activities.

By Christmas Day, TJ had started to solidify his spot as one of the top prep players in the city. He was happy and his mom was overjoyed to see him happy. This had been a long time coming.

"TJ, Merry Christmas!"

"Merry Christmas, Mama."

"I have gifts for you and your brother."

"Let me guess. Pajamas from Target."

"Surprise! There are more gifts under the tree. We even have gifts from Cajun. Check that out!"

Lindar and TJ laughed and hugged. For the first time in a long while, it seemed like everything was going to be okay. TJ thought back to last year when money had been tight and his mom had just enough money to purchase three video games. When TJ learned that his father had intercepted the mail and sold the games for crack, it spiraled him into an immediate depression. That was like the final incident in a series that made TJ really think about not having a relationship with his father.

"I know what you are thinking," Lindar said.

"Mom, it's been a rough year for us. I thought it would get better. Seems like it got worse. Why can't he stop using?"

"God only knows. I'm sure God is putting us through this to bless another family. Do you know what your middle name means?"

"Yeah, great!"

"Exactly. You are great and you will be great. You were born to do great things."

"Now, what's your Scripture?"

"Forgetting the stuff that happened before. I have to keep it moving," TJ responded.

"Forget the pajamas. You need Bible Study 101."

"Naw, Ma. That's The New TJ International Standard of the Living Word Version."

"Boy! Hush. Go open your gifts. You are absolutely silly."

TJ got out the bed, bent down and kissed his mom, and went to see exactly how much damage she had done to Target's inventory for him and his little brother

Difficult Days

Holidays were horrible for Lindar sometimes. Imagine being married, but never spending major holidays together. For three years, Lindar and Tito had not spent Christmas Day, Valentine's Day or New Year's Eve, with the exception of their wedding day, together. She got through all the holidays this year and now, on New Year's Eve, she had to get through what was supposed to be a very special day for her and her now absent husband.

As she sat in her bedroom getting Benjamin dressed, Cajun came in and took over getting him ready for the day. Lindar adored watching Cajun brush her son's hair. These two had a very unique bond, almost as if Cajun was sent to be a father to Benji. Lindar went into her bathroom and fixed her curly weave. She put on her Milani-made face within an hour. Even if she felt bad, she was not about to look like it.

Lindar appeared ready to go, dressed in all black from her hooded dress to her black suede boots, which were adorned with zippers and silver metal buckles. Cajun saw her and began to wonder exactly how many dimensions there were to her. She seemed to ease from professional to urban glam, right before his eyes. When Lindar looked at everyone ready to go, she noticed how they were all coordinated in black, gray and white—like it was all part of a plan.

To her, Cajun always looked nice. He made sure that when he got dressed for the day, you didn't want to take your eyes off him. It was more than just his warm, southern accent. It was how he walked across a room with a smoothness that made Lindar lose focus many a day. His fashion style was always unique and it was beginning to rub off on her sons. Lindar remembered years ago when she saw him and wondered why he had on this particular pair of athletic shoes with this bright orange shirt. Clearly, they did not match. Cajun had to inform her that the bottom of the shoe was orange, and the outfit would match as he was walking.

Whenever they went shopping, it would be Cajun who would pick out their outfits. Many times, TJ and Lindar would be weary of Cajun's choices. But once TJ put on one of the outfits, it was like Lindar's son had just stepped out of the pages of *GQ*. Benji was taking note and only wanted to wear his black socks with his black shoes. Right now, the term to use was "swag" for a man who could catch someone's attention. Cajun definitely had it and it was presented to Lindar on a daily basis.

"Okay den, Ma! I see chu'!" Cajun said.

"I see you, too, looking like Sean John should be checking for you."

"Damn, Lindar! I ain't know you had it in chu'!" Cajun exclaimed.

Blushing, Lindar replied, "See Cajun, you think you know me. But you have no idea."

"Well, show me what chu' werkin' wit?"

"Boy, stop. We ready to go?"

"Darlin', you mean are me and you ready?"

"What's that supposed to mean?"

"Ma, we just got called in for practice. Nana called and she wants Benji to come to the Brownhouse." TJ said.

"Practice? Brownhouse? What about me? Today."

"Luv, I'll be with you today. After I visit with my daughter, it'll be just you and me."

"I just thought we would all be together today."

"They have other stuff to do. You'll be okay, Lindar."

"Ma, we'll all be here tonight."

"Okay! We are having company tonight. The word on the street is that Cajun is cooking. Plus, your aunt and uncle are coming over, too."

In her eyes, all Lindar had was Benji and TJ. Not seeing them today would make the day more difficult to bear. Maybe she leaned on them too much. She knew that soon, TJ would be going away to college. She had to let them go to grow.

On her third wedding anniversary, Lindar spent time with her parents and dropped TJ off at practice. There was no special breakfast in bed, no special lunch at her favorite restaurant, or going out to dinner with a beautifully wrapped gift in a box with a bow. Lindar was really forced to see the marriage for what it was—over.

℘

After dropping the boys off and running some errands, Lindar began to fall in a funk. She was happy that Cajun was with her, but it didn't heal the hurt. Tito had been gone since January, and not once did he call and try and make amends. He didn't call and check on the boys. It felt more and more like Lindar and the boys were simply non-existent to him.

Instead of making the most of the present situation, Lindar just fell deeper into a dark space that she did not volunteer to try to get   out   of. Yeah, Cajun was nice and he had been good to her. It wasn't even that she wanted her husband back. It was more of a deeper hurt of a woman betrayed by the man she went to God with.

"Aw right, Luv. The boys are gone. It's just me and you. Wha' chu' wan to do?"

"Honestly? Just sleep."

"Okay, but chu' look too pretty to go to sleep. You want to go somewhere? Movies? Sumthing?"

"Naw, just sleep." Lindar responded.

"It's his loss, not churs…"

"Cajun, just give me some time. A few hours alone."

"Chu' wan me to cook?"

"No…I'm good."

"Tea?" Cajun asked.

"No."

"Lindar, I'm trying to be 'ere for chu'."

"I know, but…"

"But what?"

"You're not supposed to be here. He's supposed to be here." Lindar responded.

The tears suddenly began to fall. Cajun attempted to console her. He felt her pain and helplessness at the same moment.

"No. Cajun, just let me be."

"But chu' crying for the wrong reason. He's not out there crying over chu'. His heart ain't aching ova chu' and dem boys. Man, let him go in your heart so chu' can muv on."

"Move on to what?"

"C'mon now."

Cajun led Lindar to her bedroom. He pulled down the cover and motioned for her to sit down. He grabbed her feet and slowly took her boots off.

"Lay down, Lindar."

Lindar got under the cover. Cajun tucked her in and gently kissed her lips.

"Lindar, sometimes you have exactly what you need, exactly when you need it. You need to realize dat before it's gone."

Cajun sat on the side of the bed until Lindar fell asleep. Lindar was weighing heavily on Cajun's mind and heart. He didn't think it would go this far so soon. When they came into the house, he'd forgotten to put his phone on silent. When it started ringing, his first response was to silence it so that it wouldn't disturb her. When he looked at the missed call, he was once again reminded of his personal unfinished business.

Something About His Swagger

So many men, and boys alike, want *that* look,

That image they perceive to be "in"

When they walk by, they think people should stop and stare.

And say, "Who is he?"

Well, my man does that effortlessly.

I can be watching TV, reading or sitting.

Waiting for him to emerge,

I can only imagine other people thinking,

"Is he yours?"

It's just something about him that

Makes you stop and look back.

There are days I stop and stare,

Get completely off focus and lose my train of thought.

To be honest, a few times I was caught,

In my amazement of who he is.

His walk makes you want to talk.

His eyes make you want to shine.

And please don't let him trim up and put on an outfit.

You might not be ready for that moment.

All eyes are on him, from women and men.

He so him, he don't even see it coming.

His presence can pierce your heart with a dagger.

Believe me when I say,

It's just something about his swagger.

Unfinished Business

"Hey, Mary. Yeah, we're fine. Mia came over New Year's Day."

"And Cajun?"

"He's good. We had a good break. Now it's time to get back to school."

"How are the boys?"

"Good, real good. Girl sometimes, work is a break from home. If I fix another grilled cheese sandwich, or make another pitcher of Kool Aid, I might scream."

"I know that's right!"

"What are you and Cajun doing today?"

"Not much. He's been outside a lot, meditating with his golf ball."

"Golf ball?"

"Yeah, don't ask because I have no explanation."

"Cajun is quite interesting."

"To say the least. Let me call you after I finish up dinner."

"I gotta ask you this first. Lindar, are y'all in a relationship?"

"No," Lindar replied.

"No?"

"No, we are just friends."

"You know playing house will get you and your boys hurt?"

"Hell, so will marriage."

"Be careful, girl," Mary warned.

"I will. Love you, Mary."

"Love you, too."

The best way to end a restful break is dinner, the family, the movie The Wiz, and the sparkling eyes of a handsome man, Lindar thought.

"I got the kitchen. Go and get the boys settled," Cajun said.

"Okay, Cajun. Thanks."

"Why chu' always say my name?"

"Because I like your name and I like you. Are you leaving tonight?"

"Man…we gotta talk."

"Cool. Give me time to get them ready for bed."

Cajun had to formulate some words. He didn't know where to start. Two months turned into what felt like two years. Just last month, he was calling to check on her. Now he was caring for her, cooking dinner, running errands and contributing to the house. Her house. On top of all of that, he could tell that Lindar was happy, even while she was dealing with some serious hurt. What Lindar didn't know was that Cajun was dealing with other things. Another "her" that didn't involve her. But, since Cajun hadn't been truthful and upfront, he had to choose which "her" he wanted.

Actually, he had already made a choice. The only person who didn't know was the unchosen one: Lindar.

"The boys are knocked out. I missed the end of the movie. Can we rewind?"

"Lindar, really? It was *The Wiz*. Like chu' ain't seent it already."

"True. But since it was on and all. What's that smell? You been drinking?"

"Yea! Look, Lindar…"

"Cajun, you haven't been drinking. Why now, tonight? Are you drunk?"

"Naw! Man down!"

"Man down? What the hell does that mean? Who are you talking to like that?"

"Lindar, listen I gotta talk to chu'."

"You or the liquor? I'm going to bed."

"Naw, darlin'. I gotta get dis one out."

"Look, I have to work tomorrow. This don't feel right. The golf ball, the drinking. Are you bi-polar? On medication?"

"I'll tell chu' what, I'm not on crack."

"Ooooo! Okay! Cajun, it's like that? You on that? Not you? You didn't just say that to me."

"Lindar, listen to me please."

"Hurry up and get it out. I'm done with this conversation for the night."

"I'm going home tomorrow."

"I know that."

"No, I'm not coming back."

"Not coming back?"

"Look, this all happened so fast. You, the boys, being a family. I just…"

"Just what? Played house and now you done with us?"

"Lindar, it's not like that. I love y'all and I neva thought that I would feel like I do. The last couple of months have been good. Chu' know that."

"So, that's how you love? Damn, if only I had never answered your call. I'm so stupid."

"It's not chu. I gotta get myself together. I got some unfinished business that I have to deal with. I have to be fair to chu'. Luv, I haven't been fair."

"Being fair would have been finishing whatever you had going on before me. Never mind. We ain't together. It don't matter. Damn, I should have known better," Lindar said.

"Lindar, let's just go to sleep."

"Is she the reason?"

"*Who?*"

"Damn it, Cajun! Be honest! I went through your phone!"

"Ah! Man. Lindar, you gotta trust me."

"Really? When? When you wait for me to fall asleep so that you can call her? Or now after you're deciding you're not coming around anymore? Huh? When should I trust you? You are so full of yourself."

"It's complicated. I never meant to hurt chu' or the boys. Why'd chu' go through my phone?"

"I saw that your last missed called was labeled 'Sumthing Special.'"

"What did chu' find out?"

"Two things. It was my home number and, apparently, I'm not very special to you. Just get out!"

"Lindar, I love y'all and I really want the best for chu'. I want to be the best for…"

"For who? *Me* or *her*? Go! Please."

"I'll be back. I promise. I'll be back."

"Leave Cajun."

"Alright, can I at least hold you before I go? Don't distance yourself from me."

Lindar stood in silence, listening to Cajun, making no attempts to give in to his demands.

"Imma go. If you want me to leave tonight, I will do that. I hope you get some rest, Darlin'."

Lindar sat down on the couch as Cajun got his belongings to leave. She didn't know what to say or that anything would matter if she did say anything.

She held in her fountain of tears until Cajun walked out of the door. *How could she be so stupid, so gullible?* The tears poured for hours. She even turned off her wireless phone so she wouldn't hear his attempts to call or text her.

A year to the day that her husband had left, so had the man she had fell for at the initial sound of his voice. Her tears were warm and silent. The last thing she needed was her boys worrying about her. TJ always seemed to have a knack for knowing when the tears were falling. Tonight proved to be no different.

"Mom, why do you have your phone off? Can I turn on the lights?"

"No, honey. Go back to bed. It's late."

"Cajun texted me and told me to give you a message."

"What is it?"

"He said, 'Tell your mother to stop crying.'"

"Ugh! Go to sleep, TJ. It's getting late."

"Good night, Mommy. I wub you."

"Wub you, too. Good night."

Do She Know About Me?

Was she there for your birthday?

> That night…

>> *At midnight…*

>>> You said it was alright,

>> *In the text,*

> On the next day.

Ever since then, your text said, "Can you fit me in?"

Do She Know About Me?

She could be anyone.

From other sources, I hear I'm your woman.

Between us, we are simply friends… or *are we?*

You speak of her occasionally. It's not often positive.

She's your weakness and, in the words of Spike Lee, "You gotta have it." Ummp!

But not for long…just for those amazing moments.

Yeah!? Whatever!

Well, tell me this.

Why you portray me to be so significant, if it…didn't really matter?

Anyway.

Do She Know About Me?

About the holidays, the gifts, the late-night trips.

> You know…

>> To that place that you like to go.

Does she know how you place the world at my feet?

Now that's deep.

She's your weakness for those short moments.

I'm the one on your daily schedule.

For the life of me, why you even deal with her?

The Comeback

Months had gone by. Lindar had simply stopped responding to Cajun's calls and texts. Cajun understood and gave her the space she needed. It took him all of 24 hours to realize the mistake he had made. Some days, he wondered if TJ needed to be picked up from practice or what Benjamin wanted for dinner. He couldn't reach out to Lindar. He had hurt her too much already. It didn't take long for Cajun to get the message that responding to his calls and texts were not a priority for her.

As the days went by, Cajun tried to fill up his days with visits to his daughter and work. But, each day, the emptiness that he hadn't realized was filled by Lindar became more and more difficult to bear now that they were apart.

Lindar lost herself in teaching children at church, taking care of her sons and her writings. The more she wrote, the better she felt. She had several notebooks that she wrote her thoughts in. Some of the writings were about Cajun, but not all. She was able to share her thoughts about God, her sons and being broken. Maybe Cajun came into her life to infuse her to write. Maybe. Just maybe.

"Auntie, you have 20 missed calls and like 20 new texts," Taylor said.

"I know. I don't recognize the number."

"I'll call for you."

"No, you won't. I think it's a wrong number," Lindar said.

"Twenty times? Wait! Wait! They are calling now. Hello?"

"Taylor! Ughh!"

"Whad up, Cajun? You got some Reese Cups on ya'? What's good?" Taylor asked.

"Taylor?"

"Hold up, Auntie."

Cajun had formed a bond with the entire family. Lindar couldn't tell people what had happened between them. She knew all along that it was probably him calling. She just didn't care.

"Auntie, telephone."

Lindar was fuming. But, with all her niece had been experiencing lately, she didn't want to add to it with her problems.

"Hello."

"Hey! We need to talk. I miss bein' dere. I miss y'all," Cajun said.

"How are you?"

"I want us to sit down and talk. Can I stop by today?"

"That's good to hear. I'm fine, too."

"Stop playin', Lindar. Man! Please listen to me," Cajun pleaded.

"No, no. Thanks for calling. I have to go."

"Lindar!"

Click.

⁂

He really had a lot of nerve calling her. The only thing on Lindar's mind was the American Quilt Exhibit at the Cincinnati Art Museum. She didn't attend often, but when an exhibit would come up that sparked her interest, she wasted no time navigating Eden Park to check it out.

The last exhibit she had attended was The Gordon Parks Exhibit years ago. Lindar couldn't sew at all, but she was always amazed at what her Grandmother Helen could do with some unused fabrics. Prior to passing years ago, she had given Lindar two bags of material. She figured this exhibit could provide some well-needed inspiration.

Immediately, Lindar was in awe of the quilts on display. Some were 20-feet high. Many of them told stories of African-American and Amish cultures. Each quilt magnetized Lindar with their intrinsic geographic designs and beautiful colors. It made Lindar feel a closeness to people she didn't know and possibly would never meet.

The exhibit was small, but the displays were huge. She felt like she was surrounded by big, comfy blankets when, in actuality, they were priceless works of art.

The sun was still high outside and it was a beautiful spring day. The exhibit had attracted people of various races and cultures. It was enjoyable to be out, even if she was alone. Lindar was going to call and check on Benjamin, but decided against risking the possibility of seeing a message from Cajun. Lindar had moved on, even if only in theory.

At one of the last quilts, Lindar stopped to read the display information, when her thoughts were suddenly interrupted.

"Chu' can't be mad at me 'ere. Chu' can't run now."

"Well, I can ignore you."

Lindar continued to walk throughout the exhibit while Cajun followed her. Not once did she make eye contact with him.

"Lindar, I came to this 'ere blanket show."

"Quilt exhibit," Lindar corrected.

Cajun sighed. "I came to this quilt exhibit to see chu'. Can we talk?"

"No. I'm preoccupied with unfinished business."

"I'm sorry. I messed up."

"You are sorry. And I am busy."

Cajun walked out of the exhibit and Lindar looked at the last set of quilts, purchased a raspberry tea, and left the museum. Cajun didn't shake her because she didn't look at him—and she didn't intend to either.

That all changed as she arrived at her car to find him leaning against it.

"I need to get into my car," Lindar said.

"Not right now."

"What do you want?"

"You."

"You know what? I can't help that. Not my problem."

"Do you love me?" Cajun asked.

"Do I love you? It doesn't matter. Did you sleep with her?"

"C'mon, don't go dere."

"Oh, let's go there. Did you sleep with her? Look, I'm not the one stalking you at the museum. What? What you thought you wanted wasn't nothing at all? You got me messed up."

"Look, you have ten minutes to get it out of your system and we are going to move on from this."

"How are you going to tell me how long I have to get something out? You must think I am naïve. I'm not who you think I am, Cajun."

"So I see."

"What are you smiling for? There is nothing funny here," Lindar said.

"I've never seen you like this. You're cute when you get mad. It's kinda sexy on chu'."

"Oh! I get it! You don't want a nice woman. You want some hood ghetto chick. I think I'm gonna write a book of poetry and call it *Ghetto Chick*."

"Do you, Ma."

"Bye, Cajun. I'm going home."

"Best believe I'm not far behind chu'. I'm not letting you go this time. We'll work through the hurt."

"Cajun, why do you think this is a good idea?"

"Darlin', we want the same things. Each other. I need you. I messed up chasing after that which I don't need. Have you thought about filing for divorce from your husband?"

"No, not yet."

"Darlin', it's time for us to move on."

Cajun grabbed Lindar, hugged her and kissed her cheek.

"I'm sorry I left. Let's start new today, can we? I was talking to my mama about you today. Please give me another chance," Cajun pleaded.

Silence.

"C'mon, I came to the blanket… I mean, quilt exhibit. That's gotta say something."

"Cajun, exactly what might that say?"

"That you're special to me. Let me be the man that I can be to you. One more chance is all I ask."

"Are you done with her? Are you sure?" Lindar asked.

"I am. That part of my life is done."

"This whole situation is a book waiting to happen."

"Rock ya'self out then," Cajun retorted.

"Just maybe I will."

"You gonna forget me when the money starts coming in?"

"Depends if you can hang with me that long," Lindar snapped back.

"I got it in me."

"We'll see."

Nonstop Nonsense

After Cajun admitted to being wrong, and Lindar accepted him back, believing that all was well, she still struggled with her unhealed hurts. Besides being overweight, Lindar couldn't seem to understand why she always had problems with men. She was attractive, nice, intelligent and educated. But, she didn't attract that. She seemed to attract the exact opposite. Just maybe, had Lindar taken the time to research the hurt, she could get to the bottom of this never-ending cycle of nonsense.

Cajun really put forth the effort to reassure Lindar that he wanted to be with her. He had found a new job and was home more. He was also writing more. Lindar's heart hadn't healed from all of the men that had left her since high school. Over the years, she had fallen hard, giving her all mentally, spiritually and physically. Each man had left her. At least two went on to marry, and a total of all of them had completely erased the thought of her from their minds, including the man she shared two sons with.

What she knew for sure was that this relationship wouldn't last. Maybe earlier in her life, she had summoned the universe to cause all of this heartache. With every text and phone conversation received from Cajun, Lindar felt their "us" fading to black.

It was around this time that Lindar noticed an abrupt change in Cajun. He desired to go out and hang out with his friends more, often until some ungodly hours of the night. On several occasions, he reeked of liquor and Black and Mild cigars.

He always said, "I'm here with you. That's all that should matter."

"Yeah, only when you are actually here, Cajun."

"Lindar, if we are gonna work, chu' need to trust me and let him go."

"Have you let her go?"

"Right. Here we go."

"I'm here. Ain't that enough for you? Is anything enough for you?" Cajun asked.

"Are we getting married?" Lindar asked curiously.

"Luv, is that what chu really want? You not even divorced yet. Be patient with ya' self," Cajun stated.

"You didn't answer me."

"Let's get through your divorce first."

"Let's? Then what?" Lindar asked.

"Darlin', I'm here with you and the boys. Lindar, I'm here."

"Why?"

"Awww man! Lindar, please stop being messy."

"No, why are you here? Are we the family you wished you had with her?"

"What, you jealous?" Cajun asked.

"Get out!"

"What?"

"Get out. You don't want me. This ain't *Fantasy Island*."

"Lindar!"

"No. No. You want to be in the street. You want to be with her. I'm not what you truly want. This is just a place to stay."

"I'm going for a walk. This is too much."

"You going for a walk, or is this another excuse to hang out with your newfound friends? Be prepared to stay out."

"What's that supposed to mean?"

"You'll see."

No sooner than Cajun had left the house, Lindar had locked the screen doors and put the chain on the front door.

"Yeah, stay with whomever tonight," Lindar fussed.

Lindar grabbed several garbage bags and dumped Cajun's clothes, books and other belongings into them. Once they were all stuffed, she sat them on the side of the house.

"That'll show him."

After executing all of that energy, Lindar fell asleep, oblivious to missed calls and texts of Cajun's because she had put her phone on silent.

As she slept, she tossed and turned as if she was wrestling with something. Fortunately, her sons were not home to witness their mother melting down. Unfortunately, they would witness it for themselves eventually.

❧

The early morning sun caressed Lindar's face. Her first thought when she was completely awake was, *If only Tito had tried harder, I'd be waking up to my husband, not this dramatic nonsense.* Looking at her phone, she saw that Cajun had tried to contact her throughout the night.

Call her. For that matter, call them, Lindar thought.

It was early, but Lindar needed to walk. She needed air. Her world was closing in. She stepped into a warm bath and allowed the water to surround her with the calmness she needed. Tears fell into the water like uncontainable raindrops. She fought through those tears and got dressed. Lindar knew God loved her. But, for some reason, His love couldn't stop the pain, heartache and tears.

In the coolness of the morning, Lindar exhaled. The sun and air were the close friends she needed to be with to get the day started. She walked to the garage and instantly prayed for God to heal her heart. God was trying to speak to Lindar, but she couldn't hear Him. When she opened the door, she awakened Cajun, who apparently had spent the night in the car. He sat up and opened the door. Rubbing his eyes, he looked down to the floor.

"We need to talk," Cajun stated.

"I gotta go."

Cajun opened the door and stepped out of the car. "Gotta go where? I'm going, too."

"I have to walk. I need air," Lindar replied.

"Let's go."

Cajun led Lindar to the already opened garage door.

"C'mon. I'm walking with you. Whatever you do today, *we* do today."

Lindar walked through the door and down to the sidewalk, not saying a word.

"You locked me out. Lindar, you locked me out. I know it's hard for you. We've been at this for almost a year."

"Cajun…"

"Listen, you have to trust me, trust us, trust *this*. I wouldn't be here if I didn't want to be. We gonna get through your divorce. I promise you that."

"What about after?"

"Lindar, what about now? Don't miss *now* trying to get to tomorrow."

Silence.

"When are the boys coming home?"

"Later tomorrow."

"Then, it's all about you 'til then. Shrimp, salmon, tea and a Sanaa Lathan movie marathon. I don't care. I just need us to hang out and get through this."

"I don't know, Cajun."

"Let me show you *me*. I can't be no one else but Cajun. You first loved the voice. Now get to really know the man."

"Are you going to leave me?"

"Luv, if I've learned anything in the last 24 hours, I've learned that you'd put me out before that could happen."

"I just…"

"You just haven't dealt with your husband leaving you. To be truthful, we probably should have waited," Cajun responded.

"You're right about that, especially with you trying to get custody of your daughter."

"But now I'm here. You're here. The kids are here. We are either gonna do this or not do this."

"If we ever break up, we could never be friends again.

"Why do you do this?" Cajun asked.

"Just thinking about the possibilities, that's all."

"Let me love you. I love you and, to be truthful, I really don't know how to love. But you, I love."

"You ready to go back?"

"Sure."

Cajun grabbed Lindar's hand and kissed it.

"You going out tonight?"

"Naw. I need to work on getting us right," Cajun reassured Lindar.

"Do you really love me, Cajun?"

"More than you know. More than I can express."

"I'll try to be better."

"Me too."

"After Tito left, I didn't think I'd want to love or trust again. You have taken me off guard."

"He left. He's gone. I tell my mom all of the time how lucky I feel to have you. I have just one question."

"What's that?" Lindar asked.

"Can I bring my garbage bags in the house, and could you not put me out again?"

"I'm sorry."

"No you're not. You're hurt. Hurt people hurt people."

"True."

"We might need to talk to your pastor. We are two broken pieces, trying to fix each other," Cajun suggested.

"I feel like this is such a huge mess. I pray that it all works out."

"I pray that you see past the man that you *believe* me to be. I'm better than what you think."

"Thanks for walking with me."

"Nothing to it, Luv."

Speechless

"How long has Lindar been like this?" Mia asked TJ, who was visibly shaking.

"For about an hour or so. It all happened so fast. One minute, everything was cool. The next minute, it wasn't," TJ replied.

"Anybody call the police?"

"Naw, I don't think so."

"Take your brother and go into your room. Get Benji ready for bed. Okay?"

"Okay, Mia."

"We'll get it fixed."

"I could call Grandpa."

"Uh, no! Then we would really have to call the police."

"Maybe I should call Mary. Lindar can't go to work tomorrow like this."

TJ looked at his mother, who seemed fixed in a trance. At 16, he shouldn't have been able to see how relationships were weighing on his mom. With each event, it put TJ in a place of not even wanting to be in a relationship—now or never.

Mia began to pray out loud as her fiancé worked to secure Lindar's home.

"Lord, we ask you for guidance for this home. All that is not of you, please release it. In Jesus' name. Amen."

"Amen."

"Lindar?" Mia approached her friend slowly. "The boys said you haven't spoken in over an hour. TJ called me and we came right over."

"I wanted to call you. I couldn't. Just couldn't," Lindar responded.

"What happened here tonight, and why is he still here?"

Lindar breathed deeply. "We were arguing about money and our relationship." Tears fell from her eyes.

"Did you argue in front of the boys?"

"No. It was through texts."

"Okay. Go ahead."

"He just started saying all of these horrible things about me and my home. It hurt so badly because I've tried to stay in this."

"What did he say to you?"

"That I really don't have shit. And that, if I kept it up, he would burn down my house."

"What did you do? How did you respond?"

"I told him that he couldn't be a real man because he had never seen one, and that I would report his threats to the police if he didn't leave me alone."

"I'm sure that made him upset, seeing how he's under the radar with getting custody," Mia reasoned.

"I didn't want him to come back tonight, so I put the chain on the door. When he realized the door was chained, and he couldn't get in, he started kicking the door and the frame fell off."

"Did he come in then?"

"No, he left."

71

"But he's here now."

"Mia, right now, anybody could walk in."

"Yeah, but you could have prevented that person who damaged your home from sitting on your couch. Are you scared of him?"

"No," Lindar replied.

"I think the door will at least close for now. But you need someone professional to look at it."

"Please tell him thanks. I'm glad TJ called you."

"Lindar, I've known you since we were little girls. Cajun seems to have cast some sort of spell on you that you can't seem to break."

"I don't know what to do."

"All you can do is pray. But I'll tell you this: when he leaves again, and he will, you need to let go completely."

"Mia, I attract such craziness. I'm a mess right now. Thanksgiving and Christmas are coming up."

"Girl, there will be no Thanksgiving dinner here," Mia said.

"I'm sorry."

"Don't worry about it. I just want you to get better. You have to be better for your sons."

"Did you call Mary?"

"No."

"I'll call her tomorrow. I'm not going in to work."

"Lindar, God doesn't want you living like this in the house that He has blessed you with. This is what you work hard for. So that your boys can have the best. I know all things work … but this ain't working. Let him go in your heart."

"I love you, Mia."

"I love you too, Lindar. Please want better for yourself. Pray. Read the Bible. Turn on TBN, The Word Network or something."

"I will. All I have is my faith."

"And two boys who need their mother mentally sane. Good night."

"Good night. I'll call you tomorrow some time."

"If I don't hear from you, I'll be back," Mia reassured Lindar.

"I know."

Prepare Myself for You

(A Prayer)

Dear Lord,

    I'm having a hard time. Things aren't going the way I would like them to go. My heart aches and my self-esteem is low. Sometimes, the pain is unbearable, unmanageable.

    But I see my chocolate boys and realize that I have to keep pressing. Many people don't know how, when he left, it hurt so badly, so deeply.

    I saw my child falling and didn't know how to pull him up. The best is all I want—to move from this and rise into a survivor and a worshipper.

    My favorite day of the week is Saturday. That is when I prepare for you! On Sunday, I don't want anyone to know or see me falling apart. I want my mind and heart in the right place to teach your Word, sing your praises, and worship you unconditionally. In your presence, I want all to realize that throughout all the obstacles and pain, the most important thing for me to do is to *prepare myself for you*.

Lindar

No Thanks Here

Since Lindar had moved into her home, she always enjoyed the holidays, especially cooking her sons' favorite foods. Just the scent of glazed ham and dressing sent TJ and Benji running to the kitchen area to sample whatever was simmering.

Generally, Thanksgiving was filled with family and friends. But since Lindar's and Cajun's explosive incident, Lindar stayed very lowkey. Mia and Mary tried to reach out to her, but to no avail. Lindar didn't know how, but either her and Cajun were going to work, or they weren't going to work. Thanksgiving had become a short moment to Lindar. She just wanted to get through it.

Most days, Cajun sat around the house, trying to figure out what to do next. He realized early on how tight-knit Lindar, Mia and Mary were. He hadn't seen Mia and Mary much since early November, and he felt guilty that they didn't visit with Lindar as much. He pondered day in and day out what to do next.

How do I make this right with her? With her friends and her family? I keep messing up and I know I'm doing wrong. Sometimes, I can't leave her alone. She calls me like a drug and I go running to her, not even thinking about Lindar. Then, after I get my fix, I realize how much I love Lindar. By then, everything is messed up.

God, I wish I could do right. Me and Lindar together is either really good, or really bad. Imma try one more time. If it don't work, I'll have to do the one thing that I don't want to do to her: hurt her so bad to the point where she won't want to see me or speak to me ever again. Damn! At the rate we're going, this relationship is going down bad.

"Hey, darlin'. How was werk?"

"Good. Thanks for asking."

After a long day at school, Lindar had stopped at the grocery store. Slowly, she dragged into the house, hoping not to deal with Cajun.

"Where da boys?"

"TJ is at practice. Benji is in the car. I'll get him after I bring the groceries in."

"Naw, I got 'em. Just sit down. I got chu'."

"It's okay. I can handle it. I'm fine."

Cajun ignored Lindar and brought in the rest of the groceries. He went back out to get Benji. Lindar was amazed at how their bond had grown. Cajun was the only father Benji identified with. Cajun took a special interest in Benji, always making sure that they had time to watch TV, go outside and throw a ball, or walk the dog. If anyone tugged at Cajun's heart, it was Benji. In his eyes, Benji was his son. The only problem with that was that Cajun didn't know how to be a father, a husband or a boyfriend. In his heart, he was trying really hard to be the best he could be.

"So Lindar, Christmas is coming up. Let's start new."

"For what?"

"For us."

"Cajun, let's just try to be civil to each other."

"I know the past couple of months have been rough. Let's start over."

"It seems like that happens once a month," Lindar countered.

"When is your divorce final?"

"Next week. That's the last court date."

"Cool. I'm going wit chu'."

"You don't have to."

"Yea, I do. It's the end of one thing and the beginning of something new," Cajun responded.

"I can't deal with you right now. Not now."

"I'm sorry, Lindar. I've done you wrong. I've cheated on you. Knocked your door in and blamed you for Helena."

Cajun's words just fell into Lindar's lap, like a beautiful unwanted puppy. It sounded good, but was too much for her to handle in the moment. Looking at Cajun and listening to him made her tired.

"After all of that, we are still together. That has to say something."

"It does."

"Not now. Just listen. I don't handle stuff well. The door. Man! Imma live with that. Helena?"

"Naw, Cajun!"

"I gotta deal with it. What I did was on me. I love my daughter. I got overwhelmed. You were distant to me. I just thought…"

"You're so wrong, Cajun. If I love you, then I love her. I worked to get her just as hard as you did. You made that decision."

"I know we can get her back."

"*We?*" Lindar asked.

"I can get her back."

"This is too much."

"Lindar, look. Christmas is coming. Your divorce is next week. We can do this. I know we can. By spring we'll be ready."

"By spring, I'll be gone, Cajun. Look, just do what you need to do to get Helena. Don't worry about me," Lindar said.

"We can go to New Orleans on spring break and come back with the same last name. Chu' hear me?"

"It's too late for that."

"Whad I know about us is that it's never too late. No matter the situation or circumstance, we are joined at the heart. I got something for you," Cajun said.

Cajun went and found a neatly wrapped gift and placed it in Lindar's hands.

"Open it," Cajun said.

Lindar hesitantly began to open Cajun's gift. After pulling through the silver and lavender wrapping paper, she rested her eyes on a brand new state-of-the-art video camera.

"Thank you."

"I knew chu' would like it. Chu' can take pics, make a video or make audio recordings. It has a built-in editing system. Chu' can create your own projects."

"Really? What made you buy this?" Lindar asked.

"Because you have a gift—not only to write—but to see what others refuse to see."

"Cajun…look…"

"Don't say nothing. Let me try and fix this. Please, Lindar? I'll go to church and get serious about…"

"About what? Cajun, I may seem naïve, but I'm more complex than you see. The camera is nice, but so is my front door, my friends, my sons and my heart."

"I don't want to argue," Cajun responded.

"We're not going to. I have stuff to do." Lindar retorted.

"Deal with me, Lindar. I'm right here."

"Cajun, Christmas is coming up, and I just want my home peaceful for my sons. No arguing. No fighting. This divorce is almost final and TJ don't need another thing to be stressed about."

Lindar left Cajun in the kitchen and went to do all she knew to do: pray. Within the past year, The Serenity Prayer and *The Prayer of Jabez* had become her refuge.

"Lord, please bless me indeed and restore me. You make all things new."

Not At Christmas

December was welcomed by Lindar, as if it was the most anticipated gift under the tree. Her November was packed with seasonal events. TJ was doing well in school and sports. Benji was almost ready for preschool. Helena was still a thought of "what could be." Cajun had made amends with Lindar's friends and spent each day trying to show Lindar that she was the one and only for him.

"Hey TJ, what's the plan for Christmas break?" Lindar asked.

"Practice, practice and more practice."

"What days do you practice?"

"Every day, except Christmas Day."

"Seriously?"

"Seriously, Ma. Sometimes I wish that…"

"That you didn't play basketball?" Lindar asked, cutting TJ off.

"Naw, Ma. Never that. The court is where I deal with my stress. If I couldn't play ball, it would be like you not teaching or writing. I need ballin' in my life."

"Well, Christmas is going to be different this year. What do you want this year?" Lindar smiled as she handed an envelope to TJ.

"What's this?"

"Mo' money! Mo' money!"

"From where?"

"Let's just say I'll be writing more often."

TJ opened the envelope and pretended to faint.

"Boy, you a mess! Give me that envelope," Lindar said.

"Ma, I can't breathe! I can't breathe!" TJ lay on the floor and Lindar couldn't stop laughing.

"Ma, what did you write? Did you see this check? Did you add something to the Bible? Webster? The Constitution?"

"No, silly. I wrote a series of study guides for some books I read with my class. I sent them to the book publisher and they expressed interest in all of them."

"How many did you write?"

"I wrote three and I have four more to do."

"What happens after you write the four other ones?" TJ asked.

"After each two, I get another check."

TJ walked away from his mother.

"Where are you going?" Lindar asked.

"To get your laptop. I'm going to Disney this summer."

The money from her writings was a welcomed blessing. Lindar had managed to keep things afloat and it felt real good not to struggle at Christmastime.

ॐ

She didn't tell Cajun about the money. But he noticed a change in her. To him, it was good to see her happy. The relationship was heading in the right direction. He knew when to give her space, though. He didn't want to mess anything else up. Though, he knew at any given moment, it was a possibility.

Christmas break had started. Lindar, Mia and Mary kept in touch with all of their holiday festivities, and TJ was constantly at practice. Everything, including her writings, kept Lindar busy. It took her mind off the past hectic months.

Lindar's relationship with Cajun had taken a calmer tone. It wasn't that things were so much better, but rather that things weren't so bad. Cajun had done an honorable thing by Lindar before Thanksgiving. He went with her to her final divorce proceeding and witnessed the end of a long, stressful process.

Afterward, he wanted to go to lunch and celebrate. But all Lindar wanted was a quiche and latte from Panera Bread. Once home, Lindar went to her room and worked on finishing the study guides. Cajun didn't know how to take Lindar. She wasn't evasive and definitely not accessible to him.

❧

Later that evening, he bought dinner for the family. Even if it was a quiet celebration, it would be a celebration. Cajun knew the divorce had crushed Lindar's spirits about relationships. He somehow wanted to contribute to a peaceful day for her.

"Cajun, I'm going to pick the boys up."

"From where?"

"My parents, and Walnut Hills High School."

"I got it."

"No, it's okay. I need to run to the store so I can cook."

"No, no Luv. You go and spend time alone. Drink some tea. Get in that spa tub. I'll be back. And I know we've been having a hard time, but let's enjoy today."

"Sure," Lindar conceded.

"Sure?" Cajun asked.

"Yeah, sure."

"Okay, den."

"Well, I'll just hangout 'til you come back. You better take care of my babies."

"You know it. Lindar, what's the plan for Christmas?"

"Meaning?"

"Just wondering."

"I plan to clean up and decorate. TJ has a list. I need to make one for Benji and, of course, some girly stuff for your daughter. Cooking. Visiting family."

"Whoa! You have a lot going on there."

"I generally do," Lindar responded. "Christmas is all about Jesus and the children. What about you?"

"I ain't thought about it. Christmas has never been huge with me."

"Oh! Hmm."

"Never really had the money or the celebrations like you plan," Cajun confided.

"It's always been like that for me. Ever since I can remember. I give my boys the same traditions I had as a child."

"Are we exchanging gifts?" Cajun asked.

"Sure, I mean we can." Lindar responded.

"Sure?"

"We can. What do you want?"

"A watch," Cajun replied.

"Okay."

"And you?"

"I don't know. It's been years since I got a gift from a man. I guess whatever you get me."

"That's not telling me much."

"Whatever you get me will be nice."

Cajun left the conversation, sensing that Lindar was being passive. He didn't feel as if she cared or was giving much thought to him. He felt something he had never felt before. He wondered if she knew or suspected anything. He'd been careful with contacting his other "friend." It wasn't serious between them. He just talked to her. But, to Lindar, it would be a final blow.

❧

Sitting at home flipping through some magazines, Lindar spotted Cajun's gift. She had the money. He was trying and they were still together. He would love his gift. It would complement his style. She looked up the number to a local jeweler and placed a call.

"Hello. Do you carry Movado watches?"

She ordered the gift as Christmas quickly approached. She had raided Target and made sure that everyone had the proper PJ sets, games and toys. Her grocery shopping was systematic so that she would not get caught up in the holiday crowds. During all of this, she failed to notice that she had not included Cajun in her holiday process. He felt like he wasn't a part of her holiday plans.

"Hey, Cajun? You want to go to the movies on Christmas Eve?
TJ is going on a date. I figured we could find a movie, too."

"Naw, I'm good. Ain't nothing I want to see."

"You want to go to dinner?" Lindar suggested.

"Lindar, you just shut down Kroger. I'm sure we have food 'til Easter. Where's Benji?"

"At the Brownhouse. He's staying with my sister tonight."

"Can I give you one of your gifts now?" Cajun asked.

"No! At midnight."

"Lindar, please? And you can give me mine at midnight." Cajun said as he left the room and returned with a huge gift basket. "I had this created just for you."

"Oh my God! Cajun how did you know?"

"Because I listen to you."

Tears began to fall as Lindar went through the box. It was filled with everything lavender. Soaps, candles, lotion, oil, a small potted plant and even specially-made lavender cupcakes and cookies.

"Cajun? Thank you. Where did you find lavender cupcakes?"

"I was watching *The Food Network* and this shop in Cleveland, called *Cocoa and Honey's Cupcakes*, sells them. I ordered them just for you. I want you to be at peace today. I have something else for you later."

"Thank you!" Lindar gave Cajun the hug he had longed for the past few months. It felt so good to be appreciated by her.

☙

The rest of the day, Lindar planned her meals and planned to take TJ on his date. Cajun was just hanging around the house. It felt like he wanted to tell Lindar something, but he said nothing.

"Hey Cajun, I'm taking TJ to the movies. I'll be right back. You need anything while I'm out?"

"Naw, I'm good."

"Everything okay?"

"Yeah. It's good."

"Okay. I'll be back in an hour."

Lindar dropped TJ and his date off at the movies, half wishing
TJ had his license so that she wouldn't have to come back out. *Maybe Cajun would come and get them later,* she thought. An uneasy spirit came over Lindar. She became inclined to call Cajun. He didn't answer. The closer she got home, her mind became clouded, like God was preparing her for disappointment.

When Lindar opened the door, the emptiness smacked her in the face. All the lights were out and the stillness swept over her.

Lindar replayed the scene. She had been shopping for Christmas Day. Cajun had been pacing the house all day. Maybe he had a gift that he didn't want her to know about. He must've found the perfect gift for her. This was their second Christmas together, so he knew her pretty well by now.

She had prepared a wonderful meal for their first real Christmas together. Last year, they were just friends. But soon, they would be married. Lindar had begun to settle in, doing all the preparations she did not get to share in with Tito, including cooking, decorating and buying gifts. The excitement overcame her whenever she thought of his reaction to the engraved Movado watch she had purchased as his gift.

Upon returning home, Lindar had an uneasy feeling. A still emptiness met her at the door. On the microwave was a note that read,

I'm going home for Christmas.

Not Christmas! What about me, the boys, dinner? Damn, the watch. She went to call him or text him. Realizing that her version of Christmas was ruined, she glazed the ham, set the oven timer and turned   on The Word Network.

Where is Pastor Jamal Bryant when you need him? she thought.

Don't Call It a Comeback

With each text and smart phone alert, Lindar became overly anxious that Cajun would contact her. She knew they would have to face each other eventually. The boys thought that Cajun had simply gone home to visit his family in New Orleans for the holidays. Under the tree, they found video games for TJ, and remote-controlled cars and trucks for Benji. This was a welcomed surprise for two boys who longed for gifts from their own father.

Lindar dared not let on that she was hurt and disappointed that Cajun had simply up and left, without one single mention or hint of his departure. But today was Christmas, Jesus' birthday. There was French toast to bake and honey ham to eat.

Cajun woke up many miles away, wondering if the boys liked their gifts, wishing he could soothe Lindar's pain. He had left all his gifts to them under the tree, with the exception of a beautiful tennis bracelet that would have been so beautiful against her mocha latte brown skin. That gift, along with the Movado watch, would never be seen by their intended owners.

It would be real easy for Lindar to be upset, but God had been good to her and her family. Because of that, she was going to enjoy her day and just be happy.

"Hey, Ma! How was your Christmas?"

"Good, and yours?"

"Mama, prolly one of the best ever."

"That's the pajama effect," Lindar replied.

"Ma, we get them every year," TJ said.

"Exactly! What would Christmas be without them?"

"Christmas without PJs from Target."

"Shh! There'll be no such thing."

"When Cajun coming back?" TJ asked.

"In the next couple of days," Lindar responded.

"Cool."

"Why, what's up?" Lindar asked.

"He bought me this game and I wanted to play him."

"Oh!"

"You talk to him today?" TJ asked.

"No, I didn't answer my phone."

"That's weird. That's not like you."

❧

Days later the phone rang and Lindar ignored it. TJ stared at his mom. "You gonna answer it?"

"I hadn't planned to," Lindar responded.

"Ma, it's Cajun," TJ responded. Lindar reluctantly answered.

"Hello."

"Hey, luv."

Silence.

"I'm outside," Cajun replied. "I wanted you to know that I was coming in the house."

"Okay."

Cajun walked into the house. Lindar didn't look at him. Cajun could feel her hurt, like it was his own.

"How you been?"

"What? This past week? Fine," Lindar retorted.

89

"Where are they?"

"In the back, playing video games. They want to see you," Lindar said as she got up from the couch and walked to the kitchen.

"Lindar, listen to me," Cajun pleaded. "I had a lot going on. It was too much to handle. I had to get away. I'm here sometimes, and I don't feel like I do enough."

"So you leave at Christmas?" Lindar said as tears began to fall. "Without telling me that you are leaving?" "Is that how you love me, Cajun? Is that how I get handled?"

"There's more, Lindar. I need you to listen to me. I did leave and I regret that decision. I'm here for New Year's. I promise. I got overwhelmed and scared to tell you."

"Tell me what? Please not her again."

"I have to get some things in order for Helena. Got a court date coming up and I have to find a place to stay."

Just when Lindar thought the situation couldn't get any worse, the pain and tears took over her entire being.

"What? I don't understand."

"Luv, it's for the best," Cajun reassured Lindar. "I'll still be living here, but I have to prove stability by having a job and stable housing."

"Says who?"

"My caseworker. I'm not leaving you. I'm still in this relationship. I ruined Christmas, but I'll make New Year's right. I talked about you to my mom during the whole visit."

Lindar sat back down on the chaise lounge, not believing all this was happening. She needed to sit more for support than for comfort. "Cajun, maybe we should just separate for good. Start over with new people."

"I only want you. I've messed up a lot with us, but I swear I just want to focus on our family. The boys, Helena, and me and you."

"How about we cut our losses and keep it moving? We've been through too much."

"Lindar, go the distance with me. Don't let go now. The past year has shown me that you are what I need," Cajun said, as he sat at the foot of the chaise lounge and held her hand.

"Lindar, TJ and Benji mean the world to me. I know I'm hard to deal with. I need help with Helena. I couldn't say that at first. I need you and I need our family."

"Just give me time to sort through all of this," Lindar responded.

"Take your time, darlin'. Everything that I have ever envisioned is right 'ere. No, I don't always handle you well. I ain't never met a woman like you. I don't even know what to do with you. But I'm trying."

"Cajun, you left us."

"Not like you thinking. I went to visit home. I needed to be home and feel some stuff out. But believe me. I love y'all. Christmas would have been down bad if I would have been here. I'd just been sitting around, wondering where I fit in."

"Hmmm..."

"Lindar, let's keep moving. Or at least say you'll try."

"Cajun…I don't know. In little over a year, we have had way too much drama between us."

"I know my role in it. Let's try again please, Lindar."

"I don't know if my heart is completely there. I'm going to try but…"

"That's all I ask of 'chu."

That Day

As was her habit, Lindar woke up early in the morning to prepare tea and turkey bacon. Upon entering the room, Cajun caught her eye as he was wrapped in his cocoon watching TV.

"Luv, come lay with me."

"Why are you still up?" Lindar asked, surprised to see him up.

"I've never went to sleep. I was up all night thinking."

"You really don't like going to court. Are you ready to face all of those people this afternoon?"

"Man, I did everything those people wanted. I got a job, an apartment and daycare. I just want my child."

Cajun thought back to when his daughter came home for the holidays a few months ago. He always regretted the decisions that he had made that weekend. The responsibility was overwhelming. It's hard to be a father if you were never taught to be one. Independence was what he wanted to show. But, by the fourth day, it became too much for him.

Instead of being a truthful, honest man, Cajun led everyone to believe that Lindar was the reason that his daughter no longer lived with them. It was just another event that drove them further and further apart.

Cajun wrapped Lindar in his arms under the cover. Energy between them couldn't be denied. They tried to explain it to other people, why they couldn't part, couldn't release each other from each other. It couldn't be explained, described, defined. It just *was*.

"Lindar, I have to do things before court. Can I use your car? I will take you and the boys to school."

"Well, hurry up. Get up. You have to do something about your hair."

"I know, right. I have been untwisting all night."

"Really?"

"You messy early in the morning. I want it to grow, but I can't go to court like this."

"I am just saying," Lindar said. "You need to do something about your…"

Cajun took the cover off Lindar and exposed her to the cool morning breeze. They laughed as they played around before beginning to get dressed. Neither realized this would be one of their last laughs together for a long time.

Cajun was trying to change for Lindar and the children. He was realizing that she truly loved him. Just thinking about how she loved him often amazed and startled him. He hadn't been the best man he could have been to her. Over the past months, he said some things to her that were cruel and degrading. Cajun had Lindar in tears and often overwhelmed her with disappointment. Even when he called her pastor to inform him how Lindar was living, she managed to forgive him and love him through all of that.

"Don't forget I get off at 3, while you are running around the city."

"Lindar. I really love you. You know that. I am going to change; watch me."

Silence came over Lindar. Lindar wanted to believe Cajun, to trust Cajun. So much had happened since the summer. She was beginning to realize that if it didn't get better, it would have to end.

"I just want you to be honest with me and true to me," Lindar stated. "You have a lot going on in your life. Just be true to me."

"I am. I promise," Cajun reassured Lindar. "But you have to learn how to control your emotions. Sometimes, you get mad over nothing. You worry about the wrong shit."

As Cajun drove Lindar to work, they held hands, almost as a symbol of an attempt to hold on to each other. Cajun pulled up to the door of Lindar's job to drop her off, as Lindar stared into his eyes.

"I know you are trying. And I know once you get your daughter, we are going to be okay. I know you are trying to change for all of us."

"I am, Lindar. You will see."

"See you later."

Lindar walked in the building, thinking about the past couple of weeks. He had been attentive to her and the boys. He was making an effort. She couldn't deny that.

Once she reached her classroom, she pulled out her phone and sent him a text.

I do see a change in you.

છે

Teaching high school students with a myriad of problems is not always easy. Before you get to the academics, you have to deal with family, friends and relationship issues. This was Lindar's first year teaching high school and she wasn't sure she was cut out for all of this stress. This particular day went rather smoothly and, after an interesting meeting, Lindar was ready to call it a day.

Cajun texted Lindar:

I am running late.

Okay! I have a meeting.

When? You want me to watch Benji?

No, the meeting is now. See you when you get here.

I'm here.

Okay.

Lindar was looking forward to the shrimp dinner Cajun had promised her. Since her birthday, Cajun had made it a point to get Lindar breaded shrimp from Hook's in Bond Hill.

"Before we go home, I need to get the keys to the apartment. Do you mind?"

"No, let's get Benji first."

Lindar went inside her parents' home to get Benji. She stopped and spoke to her neighbors, who had watched her grow into the woman she was now. Cajun watched Lindar and noticed that she seemed happy and at peace. How was he going to tell her what he had been thinking since court?

৵

"Alright, Cajun. Here is the plan. You have to take three months of parenting classes and we will have to discuss setting up visitation," his daughter's case worker explained.

"Three months?" Cajun asked, stunned.

"Yes, we believe you need to learn how to interact with your daughter. Even if you and Lindar are together, Helena is your primary responsibility."

"I did everything you told me to do. I got the job, the apartment... everything."

"Well, to be honest, you should have had that anyway. You need to be stable and responsible for yourself, Lindar, and the children."

Cajun pulled into Lindar's least favorite hamburger joint and asked Lindar what she wanted. Shrimp was apparently not on the menu.

After ordering and receiving the food, Cajun headed west on Mitchell Avenue. Lindar had been in this area in passing. She never thought she'd have a boyfriend to visit in that particular area. She could see that Cajun was excited about having his own place.

The drive home was normal for Lindar. Little did she know that her night would be full of tears and lack of sleep.

Once settled at home, Lindar went to check her email and blog account. Lindar had started blogging in December and loved every minute of it. Her fingers glided across the keys to the sites of her desires.

Cajun walked into the room, reeking of smoke. Lindar had no idea what was coming.

"You know what, Lindar? I think I am going to take your advice."

"Really, what's that?" Lindar asked.

"I ain't going to deal with no women while I work on getting my daughter."

Warm tears began to form in Lindar's eyes. She turned to Cajun and the hurt in her eyes pieced his soul.

"We've been together for almost a year. I'm losing friends over this! Can't teach or sing at church over this! So you have been this nice to me to do this?! I guess the past two days have been your going away party."

"Lindar…stop…listen to me," Cajun pleaded.

"Go to hell, Cajun! You know what you're doing. This ain't about Helena or me. You are selfish! This entire time, you haven't worked and now you got a job and a place to stay…and you break up with me? Fuck you!"

"Lindar!"

Suddenly, the blog meant nothing. Lindar didn't even know how she ended up on the chaise lounge in the living room. All she knew was that she could not control her tears. Cajun sat with her and put his arms around her.

"I don't want you to cry," Cajun said. "I just need to get stuff together. In three months you'll see…I am doing this for us."

"Please leave me alone. I just need to be alone."

"Luv, save your tears for when you really need them."

"Go to hell! You can't mandate when I cry. Go next door. Go smoke some more…just leave!"

The tears fell harder and Lindar could do nothing, but curl up under the blanket.

"I can't. I don't want you to cry. I just want to work out. Everything will be okay for all of us."

"Cajun, please let me be."

Lindar pulled the blanket over her face and tried to control her tears. She had to get herself together before TJ came home.

Lease

Cajun didn't know what to do or say to Lindar all evening, so he said nothing. He remembered when he had first met her that day in the spring several years ago.

She had a light in her eyes of determination and success. At that time, she had a B.A. and was working and taking care of TJ. Years later, she earned her master's degree in education and had been teaching for some time. Now, almost a decade later, she was setting out to embark on a new adventure by creating her own publishing company, Lindar Publishing, Inc.

Cajun realized that he didn't have much to offer her, but a warm bayou accent and some occasional gifts he copped for her and her   sons. He often felt worthless, as if he didn't measure up to her. With Lindar's putting him out once a month, it didn't help the situation either. So now that he had resources, new friends and a place to stay, he figured he didn't need her as much anymore. That was the bottom line.

TJ still needed to eat and it took all the energy Lindar had to cook dinner. It was so important for TJ to have a normal home, since his father had left a couple of years ago. Lindar's and Cajun's situation was not weighing too well with him. Some of the things Cajun did and said to Lindar was causing T.J. to show that he was more than a prep school basketball star. He had hood in him and, slowly, it was seeping out.

As TJ entered the house, he could sense something in the air. Cajun was on the chaise lounge, watching the news and his mother was finishing dinner.

"How was practice?" Lindar asked TJ.

"Good."

"Y'all have a big weekend coming up."

"I know we have games on Friday and Saturday. How was your day?"

"It was okay. It could have been better."

TJ thought, *Yeah, I bet. What he do now? He better leave and not come back. He ain't half the shit he act like he is. Yeah he was cool in the beginning...now he upsets her more than my dad did.*

TJ didn't even acknowledge Cajun's presence. He grabbed a plate of food and went to his place of solitude to stuff his face and fall asleep. Normally, he would play with Benji. But for all intents and purposes, he passed out on the bed after his last bite. Benji fell asleep minutes later.

Lindar cleaned up the kitchen, lifted up all forty plus pounds of Benji, and headed for bed. As she lay in the dark, she envisioned her life without Cajun. It had been over a year since Cajun had come into her life during the separation from her sons' father. She really appreciated all that he did for her. So many chores and errands that Lindar hated to do, Cajun would pick up the slack. All it would take is one slip up, and Lindar would have his bags packed and on the porch.

It wasn't a control issue. Lindar knew what she wanted and what she wanted her boys to see. So when Cajun would spend his days outside, from evening to the early hours, running the streets drinking and smoking, he could be assured he had to leave for a few days. She really wanted Cajun to see her side of things, and try to come to a happy medium. It never happened. More and more each day, Lindar felt low on the totem pole in his life. Cajun's logic was as long as I come home to you, and share what I have with you, it shouldn't matter what I do in the streets.

Lindar laid there for several minutes and was startled when Cajun came to tuck her in for the night. She immediately pulled away and rejected the offer. Any other night, she would welcome the offer and lay in his arms until she fell asleep. Tonight was the beginning of her getting used to that not happening anymore.

∾

"Hey, I'm home." Lindar found Cajun playing video games in TJ's room.

"Guess what? I signed my lease and got my keys today," Cajun informed Lindar.

Lindar's mind came back to reality. "So, you moving in tonight?"

"No, lights don't come on till Monday."

"Really? So, I guess you'll be out on Monday and my keys will be left on the counter?"

"Lindar, you always got shit on you. This ain't the end of us."

"The hell it ain't. You got a place to go, so go," Lindar demanded.

"What you mad you can't put me out?"

"What?"

"You can't put me out anymore. Can you?"

"Get out of TJ's room! You are pure evil." Lindar screamed.

"Lindar, what is wrong with you?"

"You are no better than my ex-husband."

"So, what does that say about you?"

"That I don't make good choices."

❧

Grabbing her things, Lindar decided to attend a gospel concert prior to the basketball game. If Lindar needed anything else right now, it was Jesus and some gospel music.

The concert was wonderful. It was hard to believe that some teenagers just delivered a concert like they were the opening act for Fred Hammond. My niece has such a beautiful voice. It was as if her notes hit the ceiling in the Walnut Hills auditorium.

"You enjoy the concert?" Ney asked afterward.

"Yeah, Ney. It was wonderful. Y'all really did it on 'I Will Bless the Lord.' I loved that."

"Well, now it's time for some hoops."

TJ was playing basketball only several steps away. After the game, it was off to McDonald's and then home. After the game, we headed up Montgomery Road to the McDonald's in Norwood.

"Can I have six double cheeseburgers, three fries, and a caramel latte? Oh yeah! And two large orange drinks with no ice."

"Do you want the double cheeseburgers or the McDouble?"

"Double cheeseburgers."

"You know the McDoubles are ninety-nine cents. The double cheesburgers are ten cents extra," the cashier said.

"Yeah. I know. I saw the special on ABC Nightly News. Now, can I have six double cheeseburgers please?"

"For your latte, do you want whole milk or skim milk?"

"Whole. For the love of God!" Lindar exclaimed.

Lindar's day seemed to get longer and longer.

"Hey, Cajun. I bought you something to eat."

"I already ate."

"Really. What did you eat?"

"What difference does it make?" Cajun snapped.

"Well, normally when you go out to eat, you get food for the boys. But I guess things are changing for real."

"Whatever." Cajun attempted to go back to sleep.

"Make sure you set your alarm because I am not taking you to work in the morning."

"A'ight."

Lindar searched through his coat and took her keys. She found the parking ticket for her car.

"Damn it, Cajun! You could've paid this.

Alarms rang thoughout the house. Lindar made sure that Cajun was awake. Prior to leaving out, he asked Lindar for the keys.

"Did you take the keys?"

"Yes, and you are not getting them back. On your way out, don't knock anything over."

Those Damn Text Messages

Cajun had an ugly side to him. If he was really upset with Lindar, he wouldn't say mean things to her; he would text them. He seemed to know exactly what to say that would set her off. Lindar's Scorpio nature would kick into high gear and, before you know it, there would be a war of words. The difference between Lindar and Cajun is that Cajun seemed to want to inflict pain with his words that were hard to heal from.

Lindar could memorize those texts with just one reading, or she would save them in her phone. After Cajun had calmed down, he would act as if nothing had happened and he would be upset when Lindar repeated some hurtful phrase he had sent her. If Lindar wasn't paying attention, Cajun would delete all the messages out of her phone in hopes of starting anew. That was difficult for Lindar because she didn't know how to let those cruel, mean words go.

Now that he was leaving, she was beginning to miss him already. Her spirit told her to reread those messages he had left for her over the past couple of months, and determine if she still missed him.

➤ *Ok I'm just going to come over there. Don't be mad cause I don't wont u, let me get mine.*

➤ *Man who the fuck u thank u talkin' to I ant fucking with u at all . Got it I'm tired of playing with u.*

➤ *Go head couse i dont wont u .bitch u dumb, play with my child and u and urs well have to go in to hiding*

- Suck my dick bitch .fuck in play with my child and if its the last thang i do I'm c u.
- Mad i am fuck fat. fake ass dumb ass bitch u mad cause I don't wont u. That is all it is. fuck u.
- Couse i dont wont u .let u come up in court .and I ant going to stop tell I get u.
- Go head play. bitch u sad.
- U hard up 4 a man. r somethang.
- Ant that right. u wont to b the shit and ant got shit 4 real.
- Avery time I thank bout u it make me mad. if coude go back to the first time I seen u I woude have told u to get the fuck out my face.

- .i hope u inside crying may b u well drown ur self.
- As i set hear and thank u r the dumbes bitch I aver meet. I hate ur fuckn guts sorry u meet me u should have been a ms carry.
- And u die in ur sleep.
- Well u shoude have die the day .day had u.
- I ant naver liked u. U ms me b 4 i ms u.
- Dum bitches like u mad the world bad.
- Avery time u get mad at me u got somethang to say bout my kids bitch u a poor lead as a woman i dont need u now grow some nuts and play with them.
- Block my number . u in lov wen i play pupe. run tell that.
- The only person i had in my corner. i fuck that up .man this shit hard.

Alone

Cajun felt defeated and dejected again. He knew she would be hurt because he was moving out, but not like this. In his heart, he knew it was the best for everyone. On his way to work, and once there, he attempted to contact Lindar. Lindar was way past hurt, almost to the point of no return. She ignored the phone calls. She also ignored the texts and simply fell back asleep.

While he knew that she was the perfect woman for him, he couldn't get past his insecurities and inabilities to care for his own children, let alone her highly motivated sons. It seemed like the more he tried to do the right thing, the worse things got with Lindar.

Damn, Lindar. I know you love me, but you probably shouldn't.

I ain't what you need and only some of what you want. I need to get away from her and figure shit out in order to be the man I know I could be. But damn, I gotta hurt her to find me. I don't want to hurt her, but I gotta find me.

Mary heard her friend crying. "Lindar, what is it?"

"He's gone for good!"

"What happened?"

"TJ got called to the gym early and we had to leave and pick up Phil. I explained that to Cajun. I told him he could get his stuff tonight. Then he started sending those damn text messages."

"Are you okay? Lindar, why didn't he have his keys?"

"I took them. I knew he was leaving. He got a place to go to."

"Lindar, you can't keep taking from him and putting him out. He is not Tito. Cajun loves you and the boys," Mary said. "I know you two have strong feelings for each other, but maybe the split is good for both of you. Sweetie, I love you like a sister. You haven't healed from your failed marriage and Cajun has some decisions to make about his life, too. He has to heal also. Y'all like two wounded people trying to save the world."

Lindar wept softly in the background. She knew that Mary was right. Tito left her and the boys so much to use crack that all Lindar knew was a man leaving her. With Cajun, it was always her putting him out before he had a chance to leave her. She knew it was unfair, but she would never admit that to him. It was how she defended her heart.

"You two are very talented writers, very creative and beautiful people," Mary continued. "But this clearly ain't working. Let him find his way and you find yours. You are just a few phone calls away from a new career

Lindar was working the admissions table at Walnut with Benji when her phone went off with a text message.

"Just give me three months, you'll see."

"Three months for what?"

"For us. I promise. I love you."

"Why?"

"Cause you give me what I need."

"I don't know."

Lord, I should not have gotten involved with him. It hurts so bad to know that I won't see him every day. I am broken, but I know that he means the world to me. We have been seeing each other for over a year and now, I don't know.

I am happy that he is on his path to obtaining Helena permanently. The problem with him is that he is not always on the up and up about his intentions.

God, grant me the serenity to accept the things I can't change, the courage to change the things I can, and the wisdom to know the difference. God, I need you. This is too much for me.

ॐ

Lindar looked at her phone to see a text message from Cajun.

You get to work ok?

No, I'm running late. Where's my remote?

In the car, in the garage.

Can you get it?

No. It's dark and too early for me.

Can I get it?

Sure.

Can you take me to work?

Alright.

Lisa, Lindar's sister, had prepared breakfast in celebration of Martin Luther King, Jr. Day. After taking Cajun to work on the cold, snowy morning, Lindar came home and relaxed in her garden bath as she prepared for breakfast and a day of worship. As she enjoyed the winter morning, she received yet another text from Cajun.

I hope you got home safely. Take care, love. See you on the flip.

Cajun, what does that text mean?

It means bitch I ain't fuckin' with you no more. I got my own place now. I don't need to come around your fat ass no more putting me down.

Lindar's eyes stung with anger. *He didn't say that. I know he didn't.*

What are you talking about?

Bitch I don't want you. Fuck you with your fat ass!

I should file a restraining order on you.

Bitch, if you and me come up in court you and yours will have to go into hiding.

Checkmate.

Fuck you Lindar. What you hard up for a man? Don't be mad cause I don't want you.

What? Don't be mad? You probably never did want me. This was just a place for you to stay.

You couldn't keep a crackhead. Suck my dick.

With that, Lindar stopped texting. She had endured his abusive words through texts and she was finally worn out. Nothing left to do but to go to breakfast and to church.

In church, Lindar sat with Mary, but couldn't remember one word Pastor Mike preached about. She was happy to be sitting with Mary, who had been such a blessing to her.

"So, what are you doing after church?" Mary asked Lindar.

"Jen, TJ and I are going to see Notorious. You want to go?" Lindar asked, trying to be kind.

"No, I have a birthday party to attend. Going to the movies might make you feel better."

"Yeah! I have been looking forward to seeing this movie."

Mary's intuition told her not to mention Cajun. Not being able to place a finger on the problem, Mary knew her friend was disturbed.

❧

This particular Sunday was rainy and cold. Lindar took the expressway to the movie theater. It was only hours before she had driven the same path to take Cajun to work.

"Mom?"

"Yeah?"

"What happened?"

Lindar took a deep breath and began to tell TJ the story of the past couple of days. TJ looked at his mother as she drove across the Suspension Bridge.

"Mom, he always does this to you," TJ stated. "I don't understand why you let him come back."

"I can't explain it myself."

"Let this be the last time. If he can't do right by you, then he don't deserve you. You deserve better than him," TJ said.

"I know."

"Do you? He is wrong and you know it. He calls you bitches, tells you are dumb and stupid, talks about your weight. He pulling you down, Ma!"

"You sound like Spencer."

"I don't want to do all that now." They both laughed. "I just want you to be okay," TJ confided.

"Me, too. Let's enjoy the movie."

Alone

Breakups are hard, even when they are necessary.

In the beginning, I didn't know what to expect, how I would act.

But I am cool.

I sit sometimes and reflect on what happened.

Did he say what I think he said?

No, he didn't say that. He couldn't have meant that.

But, I go on.

On with my life, as it was before you entered.

On with raising my boys to hopefully ensure they never say to a woman a fourth of the things you have said to me in the final days.

Yeah. We had some good times, and I admit that you were a blessing for us at that time.

That time has gone.

Gone are the days of me feeling like I was low on the totem pole.

Gone are the days that I felt unbeautiful and unwanted.

Gone are the days waiting for you to find time for me, while you lived with me.

So, now, you can do as you please with whom you please, and not have to worry about me.

I will continue to grow.

Continue to seek God.

Continue to be the best mother, sister, daughter, friend.

Continue working on being the best me for everyone that I meet.

Now that I am alone.

Snow Day

"You know we are supposed to get slammed with snow tonight."

"Well, CPS rarely takes a snow day, so I am not worried."

"I don't know, Lindar. It is on the news stations that we are getting something short of a blizzard. So you may be home tomorrow with your pumpkins."

"Great! That is what I need, to be at home."

"What is wrong with you?" Mary asked Lindar.

"Nothing."

"It's Cajun? Isn't it?"

"Mary, I just need to stay busy. When I am not busy is when I think of him. I don't want to think about him. A snow day is the last thing I need."

"Have you talked to him?"

"For what? We don't have nothing to say to each other."

"Lindar?"

"Mary? We can't talk. Not now, probably not ever. I gotta go."

"Call me later."

"Okay."

Lindar sat in the dining room, dreading a day at home with no way to go anywhere. If only she could get Cajun out of her system, out of her life. As much as she tried, she couldn't shake the feelings she had for him. Cajun meant more to Lindar than any man she had been involved with over the years, including her former husband. Tito had been the love of Lindar's life. They had married, had beautiful boys and a wonderful friendship in the beginning. But crack had destroyed so much of that.

Cajun came in at a bad time. The relationship was not bad; the timing was bad. Both Lindar and Cajun were coming out of crazy, dramatic situations. They probably should have never tried to be together at that time. Hindsight is 20/20 though. Now both Lindar and Cajun were trying to find ways to nurse current and past heartaches.

"Mom, did you look outside?"

"For what?"

TJ dragged his mother to the front door and opened it.

"What the…"

Lindar's beautiful walkway and porch were already covered with inches of snow. *Impossible*, Lindar thought. *This is not possible.*

"Snow day, snow day, no school, no school," TJ rapped, as he started his freestyle session.

"Turn on Channel 19, TJ, and work on the rapping please."

"Just in: All Cincinnati Public Schools will be closed tomorrow and, with this storm moving, it may be a long week for students, teachers, and parents."

Lindar ignored all the texts and phone calls. She couldn't stop thinking about Cajun.

❧

The next morning, Lindar got up, cooked breakfast and went back to sleep. She knew this would be the perfect time to get lesson plans ready for her Praxis III evaluation or even create lesson plans for upcoming weeks. Instead, Lindar walked around her home as if she was a zombie. Lindar had been a single parent for nearly 17 years, so being alone was nothing new to her. Lindar decided to read a book, something that she enjoyed doing. After the boys had spent the morning eating and playing video games, they fell asleep for the afternoon in TJ's bed.

Several chapters in, Lindar decided to watch a movie. She turned to HBO and started searching for a movie to watch. Wrapped up in her throw blanket, Lindar's mind drifted back to days when she and Cajun would sit around and he would pick movies to watch. Cajun would pop popcorn in a pot, not in the microwave, and make sure everyone had their own separate bowl. He would always have the most popcorn of everyone sharing in the snack. Then, they would sit and watch TV together.

Tears began to fall down Lindar's face. She turned the TV off and sat and thought about those times, realizing now how important they were to her. If only he had not... but he *had*. That moment forever changed the course of their relationship.

When Lindar woke up, the snow was still falling from the previous day. Only this time, an ice storm was following it. She thought to herself, *If CPS isn't closed, I bet I won't be there.* As she reflected on her day, Lindar realized how unproductive her day had been. She looked around at her beautiful home, and it was a hot mess. The dishes were in the sink, the stove was full of pots and pans, and there were loads of clothes to be washed. Tomorrow, if Lindar was off, she would use it to do some serious house cleaning. Maybe cleaning would give Lindar what she needed: the boldness to focus on something other than her broken heart.

Ghetto Chick

Months ago, Lindar hadn't thought that *Ghetto Chick* would really come to fruition. She had written so much over the past year. She sat and read each poem on her computer. Wow! What a journey.

I can't even be mad at Cajun if this is the end result, she thought. Lindar didn't know how it was all going to come together, but she knew God had given her a vision and a voice, and she had to use it. Pastor Mike had spoke about it in Bible study: "He won't give you the vision without provision."

Cajun was not really happy with some of Lindar's writings because they spoke to their situation. Cajun was definitely a private person. Now that the relationship was over, Lindar was not sure how he would take her book coming out. But it had to come out. She had to say to the world, "I have been broken and hurt, but I am okay. And you can be okay, too."

She spent so many hours on the Internet, looking up publishers and looking into self-publishing. If no one was interested, then Lindar would publish the book herself. Selling it was going to be the easy part. Getting it printed was another thing. Google became Lindar's late-night BFF, until Lindar could not stand to even type the keys on her computer. One night, a thought was planted in Lindar's mind and it forever changed the course of *Ghetto Chick*.

It came to her to put the book together herself and send it to a local office supply store. It couldn't hurt. So, with the aid of her desktop publishing program, and her creative thought process, Lindar created *Ghetto Chick*. After days of editing and rewriting her bio, she was ready to log on to Josh's Office Supply Shop and send *Ghetto Chick* to be printed. After pressing send, Lindar eagerly awaited the email that her printing job was complete.

❧

"Hello, welcome to Josh's Office Supply. Is there anything I can assist you with?"

"I am fine. I need the copy center. Thank you." Lindar confidently walked to the copy center.

"Hi. You must be here for Lindar Publishing."

"Wow. Yeah! How did you know?"

The attendant blushed as Lindar approached him.

"It was just something about you."

"Okay! That makes me feel good."

"Here is your package. Would you like to look it over before you leave?"

"Yeah! Thank you."

Lindar opened the white and red envelope. She could not speak a word. She closed her eyes and thanked God for her parents, who had always instilled in her to reach for the stars. This was it. *This is what I was born to do. I was born to be a writer*, she thought.

"What do you think?"

"I am amazed. Thank you so much."

"Can I show you something? We have some other options for your book."

"Really? This is unreal."

"Do you have a minute?" The salesperson asked Lindar to come around the counter and look at his computer. She sat at the computer and was shocked at what the clerk had done.

"I was thinking you should go black and white because it would be cheaper," the salesperson said. "But you could go with a color cover to grab people's attention. Now, how much do you plan to sell this for?"

"I had not thought that far," Lindar admitted.

"You need to think that far. Who is your target audience? With the economy being what it is, you need to think about your cost to print and the cost to the customer."

"Well, what do you think?"

"I am thinking five dollars, maybe six. But nothing more. You will make almost a two-dollar profit off each book. With this being your first book, that will be good for you to get your name out. When your next book comes out, you can charge a higher price."

"Where are you from?" Lindar asked the salesperson.

"New York."

"You have a degree?"

"Consumer Marketing. Why?"

"You know an awful lot about pricing and what consumers want."

"Take these books home. Look them over, go to some bookstores and look at similar books. After you have done that, come back so that we can talk."

"Okay. I will do that."

As the salesperson wrung up Lindar's sale, he asked her a question.

"Do you like what you wrote? Do you think women will enjoy your writings?"

"I love what I wrote. Did you read some of the writings?"

"I did and I think you have a voice that needs to be heard."

"Thank you. I will be in contact."

"If you won't, I will. I have your email address."

"See you."

෪

Lindar could not wait to show her mother and her girlfriends what she was working on. But, at that time, Lindar did not realize that the book was not finished. She was only in the beginning stages of putting together her first self-published work.

"Mom, look at what I just got from the printers."

"The writing is small, isn't it?" Lindar's mom asked.

"Mom, just look it over."

"When does it go on sale?"

"Don't know. It is still a work in progress. I am going to the Black Book Fair and attend a publishing workshop, hosted by Valerie Lewis-Coleman."

"When is that?"

"This coming Saturday, at the Freedom Center. I am taking Ben and Taylor. On the radio, they mentioned having a kid's section. Ben will like that."

"Well, stay on course. It looks like your dreams are coming true."

"I know we deserve this."

"We most certainly do."

Upon arriving home, Lindar logged on to her computer and emailed her closest girlfriends about the day's events.

Hey Everyone,

I picked up my first review copy of Ghetto Chick *from the printer. I am sending you some of the poems. Tell me what you think.*

Be Blessed,

Lindar

❧

Sitting at the computer, Lindar pulled up *Ghetto Chick* and thought something was missing. She needed to figure it out soon. Her mind went to Cajun. *I hope you don't see my name in lights and wish that you were mine, so that you can shine. If this really happens, you had your hand in it. But you have made your decisions. I am not dumb and stupid. Maybe I couldn't keep a crackhead. Maybe I couldn't keep you, but I will rise up and above the ashes. Watch me flow. You gonna see. You messed up with me.*

❧

"Lindar, you never told me you were a writer."

"It is just something that I do, Peaches."

"This book is what is needed for our teenage girls to have a discussion. This book is bigger than what you think. No one is speaking like this to women about their situations. When you get it together, I want to use it."

"Thank you, Peaches. That means so much to me. I have been through it this past year and *Ghetto Chick* kinda sums it up. Thank you for encouraging me. I am so glad we met."

"God has His hand on you and your family. He has His hand on your talent. He is going to use this for His glory. You have to believe that."

"I am beginning to realize that *Ghetto Chick* is bigger than my marriage failing and Cajun breaking my heart."

"When you are doing God's work, it is never about us."

"Thanks. I will let you know when I get it published. See you Sunday."

"Be blessed, Lindar."

Lindar had the best set of girlfriends, and meeting Peaches only added to Lindar's support circle. She and Lindar had met at church, but really became close during praise team rehearsals. Peaches was so full of life and boy, did she love the Lord! When Peaches prayed on Sunday morning, Lindar could do one of three things: raise her hand in worship, try to stop her uncontrollable tears, or simply sit in awe of how Peaches allowed God to use her.

Forgiven

I forgive you for every negative thing you said or did to us. And I hope everything was worth losing our friendship, if we were ever truly friends.

Okay. Good 4 you. Now the thought of you pisses me off. Keep all that shit to urself. Got me.

You need to forgive and be forgiven. I don't know why I piss you off. You got what you wanted. Got me. The boys miss you. Thought you might like to know.

Whatever. I can't stand you, but I do miss them.

You can call them and see them. You have been like a father to them. I can't deny that.

Where are they?

Right here.

Dear God,

I tried to do the right thing. I do forgive him. I have to in order to move on. He didn't have to respond like that. For real, he didn't have to respond like that. He didn't have to respond at all. He's so him that it's pathetic.

Gotta keep it moving. Got to do your will. If Cajun and I are meant, it is in your hands.

Lindar

Lindar sat on her bed and searched her room for answers. Staying busy was what she had learned to do. It was now well over a month since Cajun had left. Still, there were days when she felt like he would appear, like nothing had ever happened.

"Hi, Spencer. How are you?"

"Good, and you?"

"You want honesty?" Lindar asked.

"Why, auntie? Why? Let him go?"

"How are your classes? You going bowling tonight?"

"Classes are good. I have like a 3.9 GPA."

Spencer was the classic student. No matter what was going on in her life, she never let her grades suffer.

"3.9? Seriously? I didn't see those kind of grades until I went to Xavier for grad school."

"Yeah and it looks like I'll be a sophomore next quarter."

"Look at you! You are doing it real big. I am so proud of you," Lindar said.

"When is *Ghetto Chick* coming out?"

"Soon. This whole publishing thing is crazy. I spend so much time on the computer till my carpal tunnel from the 90s flares up. But I am progressing. The book itself is finished. I just edited the review copy."

"Auntie, I can't wait. You deserve what is about to happen," Spencer said.

"I think we all do. This ain't just for me. All of us worked for this."

"Have you written anything new?"

"I wrote *Run Tell That* and *Alone*."

"Okay! *Run Tell That*?" Spencer asked?

"It was a phrase Cajun would use when he was upset."

"Auntie, you deserve more than him. He will miss you more than you miss him."

"Spencer, I think that depends on the day."

❧

Since Cajun had left, Lindar had been writing like a crazy woman. Cajun had been her drive to be creative and now she had to find it within her. Writing *Run Tell That* was hard for her. Not because it made her think of him, but because she wanted it to be powerful. She wanted it to be bold and punch readers in the stomach. The poem began with him stating that he used her.

Now that you say it's over,

You got them thinking you used me.

And that's okay.

It's the only way for you to get through your day.

Lindar really wanted to make a statement with this poem.

You won't tell 'em you miss me.

How you wish you could talk to me, see me.

Tell 'em how we spent many a night writing by candle light.

Tell 'em how whatever I asked for, you would go get in the middle of the night.

Remember snacks after the act?
See, you won't tell that.

Lindar really wanted readers to feel through her words. This was her life and heart that he was dealing with. This relationship was no joke for her.

Tell 'em about the nights wrapped up in your cocoon, watching TV.
Or about those nights I let you explore me.

See, won't tell that, will you?
Say, Boo, who really used who?

Run tell that.

❧

Sitting in the living room with the candles flickering, Lindar knew that this work was not complete. She read it over and over, and realized what was missing. He had not used her; he motivated her to be better.

She picked up her pen and thought back on the days when rappers had battles without killing each other. This was a battle of the heart, and Lindar was getting ready to call Cajun out hard. With what she was thinking, he would have no comeback for this particular writing.

Or about those nights I let you explore me…

"Hmm! I am going to be okay in this. For real, Cajun, you didn't use me. You *infused* me. I am going to take your pen. You supposed to be the poet. Darling, I got something for you. Watch me flow." A powerful, creative energy came over Lindar and she wrote the final piece to her poem.

Tell 'em about the nights wrapped up in your cocoon, watching TV.
Or about those nights I let you explore me.

Cajun, you were the inspiration for this book.
Are you even going to let them take a look,
At who you really are?

You knew I was on a mission.
You knew my success would happen.
You infused me, not used me.
Hell, in the end, I took your pen.

See, you won't tell that? Will you?
Say, Boo, who really used who?

Run tell that.

Even with all the scribbles on the paper, Lindar was clear about her masterpiece. She read it over and over again. After reading it a fourth time, Lindar realized that she was on her road to healing from the hurt of her relationship with Cajun. She was pleased with this newfound knowledge.

Run Tell That

Now that you say it's over,
You got them thinking you used me.
And that's okay.
It's the only way for you to get through your day.

You won't tell 'em you miss me,
How you wish you could talk to me, see me.

Tell 'em how we spent many a night writing by candle light.
Tell 'em how whatever I asked for, you would go get in the middle of
the night.
Remember snacks after the act?
See, you won't tell that.

Tell 'em about the nights wrapped up in your cocoon, watching TV.
Or about those nights I let you explore me.

Cajun, you were the inspiration for this book.
Are you even going to let them take a look,
At who you really are?

You knew I was on a mission.
You knew my success would happen.
You infused me, not used me.
Hell, in the end, I took your pen.

See, you won't tell that, will you?
Say, Boo, who really used who?

Run tell that.

I Am Her

At the computer, Lindar created her mailing list of her closest girlfriends. Once that task was completed, she sat and autographed a copy of her soon-to-be bestseller, *Ghetto Chick,* for each friend.

This was an opportunity for her to share her passion for writing with some of her friends. She could only imagine the looks on their faces when they opened their envelopes.

Lindar knew how blessed she was to have wonderful friends who loved and supported her. They were all professionals in their own right, saved, and supporters of President Barack Obama. It was so important for Lindar to have friends with similar interests and desires.

Sitting there signing the books made Lindar feel like she was at her first book signing event. Is this what it would be like? Would her girlfriends accompany her at some of those events? What about Tito and Benjamin? Just the thought of all of the opportunities made Lindar excited and nervous.

Would Cajun come and support her? This was Lindar's final thought as she signed the last book. *I know God gave me a talent, and I will be successful. But Cajun was a part of that, too.*

∂

"Mommy, drank! Draaaaaaaaaank!"

"Okay, Benjamin."

"Drank! Drank!"

"Let me find your cup."

No matter how many sippy cups were purchased for Benjamin, no one could ever find them. It didn't help that Benjamin liked to sleep with TJ. Any given day, there would be six cups under TJ's bed.

"Mommy, do it! Do it!"

Benjamin ran down the hall with his basketball and waited for Lindar to do it.

"Introducing our starters. He's in preschool, number three, Bejaminnnnnnnnnnnnnn!"

Benjamin ran down the hall and pretended to give his invisible teammates a low five and jumped up to greet another invisible player with a bounce on the chest. After going through the motions, he started running three-year old suicides. At TJ's games, Benjamin didn't speak many words. He simply sat and absorbed every move his brother made on the basketball court. Once they got home from the game, Benjamin imitated every move he saw on the hardwood kitchen floor.

Lindar often imagined what the future would hold for Benjamin. She never imagined TJ would be playing high school basketball at his current level of success. Now, with Benjamin at the basketball court two to three times a week, she somehow knew she had at least another 13 years of basketball.

Benjamin wore himself out. After his many layups and slam dunks, he curled up in a ball and fell asleep. With him and TJ sleep, Lindar found time to simply exist in a rare and peaceful moment.

෨

She lit a candle, turned off the lights, and turned on the radio. Grabbing her throw blanket, she sat down on the cocoa brown chaise lounge. TJ was doing well in school, as was Benjamin. Lindar Publishing was slowly taking form. Everything seemed to be in motion. Her days without Cajun were becoming normal. Finally, Lindar's mind was beginning to release those negative thoughts of being called dumb and stupid. There was a part of her that knew Cajun didn't mean those cruel words, but those words had cut her spirit deeply.

Gospel music filled the air. Lindar had a love for music. R&B was fine, but gospel music got to the root of her problems. That night was beautiful. That night was peaceful. The light of the moon was shining through the bay windows—just like those nights when Cajun would hold her until she fell asleep. On this night, Lindar was not wrapped in Cajun's arms, but the arms of God. A song played on the radio. Lindar knew the artist, but had never heard the song before.

JoAnn Rosario had easily become a favorite of Lindar's since she had heard her song, *More, More, More* years ago. Her voice seemed to touch the very heart of God. This song caught Lindar by surprise. The lyrics of *I Hear You Say* flowed from the radio right to Lindar's spirit. And, as God held Lindar, she became overwhelmed with emotion and released all of the pain of a failed marriage and a broken heart. At that moment, Lindar heard God say to her, *"Lindar, you keep pressing for your goals. You will be blessed. You'll move past the pain and be healed."*

Eventually, the tears stopped and Lindar fell asleep, not realizing that God had lifted and removed a deep heartache she never realized she had.

I Am Her

Smart. Intelligent.

The one you want to spend time with.

Tall girl, sexy woman.

Listener, speaker, lover.

You looking for me?

Can't you see? I am her.

The one you want.

The one you're scared to have.

Man up. Grow up.

You know me. You love me?

I am loyal.

I am yours.

Don't you see?

I am her!

Write Through It

"T. Tash, how's little princess doing?"

"Girl, fine. How are you and the boys?"

"Girl, we cool."

"And Cajun?"

"Tash, long story short, it's over and he's gone," Lindar sighed.
It has been a rough one. Probably more so than my husband leaving."

"Lindar, how are you holding up? What are you doing to get through this?"

"Absolutely nothing. I can't think. I can't sleep. I cry. My heart hurts so bad, Tash."

"I can come over."

"No. No. I don't want people to see me like this. God, here I go again. I didn't see it coming."

"Lindar, please!"

"What?!"

"You knew he wasn't completely over her. What, he waited till you fell asleep to call her? Long distance, at that. You knew. You may not have wanted to face it, but you knew."

"But he was here with me and my boys doing what…"

"What? What their father wasn't doing? That's called playing house. If he truly wanted you, he would have asked to marry you after he witnessed the divorce was final. He wouldn't have told your pastor you all were living together, which resulted in you being sat down at church. Real talk, Lindar."

"That was a whole mess within itself."

"Yeah, one that got you sat down and a whole lot of broken stuff. Now look, I'm not going to be harsh on you. Obviously, you're going through it. What I have to say to you is coming from a place of love."

Tash got silent as she heard her friend crying.

"Lindar, when the boys' father left, he took a huge part of your heart with him. Now, Cajun has left and you have some mending to do. To begin with, the last thing you need to do is date right now. Work on a book, your blog or something. What'll get you through this is God and your writing. It's time to let both of them go in your heart and really take time out for you."

"I know Tash, I…"

"Wait a minute.," Tash stopped Lindar. "You and I both have had some difficulties, and we've supported each other. Truly understand what I am telling you. I want you to take your seeds and plant them somewhere else to grow."

"What?"

"All that you pour into relationships, pour into another area of your life. You never know. You may meet a singer from Ghana who needs a manager."

"You just have no idea what God has for you. Stop selling yourself short. Let a man find you who can match you educationally, financially and spiritually," Tash continued. "Date a brother who understands subject-verb agreement. And please stop going back to get people you left along the way."

"Tash, I don't get out much and Cajun…"

"Cajun is gone, probably back to her and living in subsidized housing. Sweetheart, that's just not who you are. God and your parents don't expect you to live in lack. Neither should you."

"Princess needs to eat and get ready for bed. Take your seeds, Lindar, and plant them elsewhere. Get your notebook and write it all out. When you are finished, read it. What would *you* tell *you* after reading your truth?"

"Thanks, Tash."

"It'll be okay in time, sweetie. Love you, Lindar."

"Love you too, Tash."

"Lindar?"

"Yes?"

"He'll find you. You're what's missing in his life. You have to be ready for that. You have to be healed for that. When he comes, you'll know. He'll be drama free and walking in God's will."

"Dating is not an option for me right now," Lindar responded.

"I know. You'll know when you're ready."

"After all you've been through, you still are able to encourage me. Amazing."

"Girl, please. That's the God in me." Both women laughed out loud for the first time in the conversation.

"Girl, bye!" Lindar exclaimed.

"See you, Lindar."

After getting off the phone, Lindar started writing about the past couple of months. As she wrote, she thought that her writing would make a cool book, kinda like the play in the movie, *Something's Gotta Give*, which was one of Lindar's favorite movies.

"Hmmm. If I turned this story into a book, I would title it, *Something Special*."

At This Very Moment

At this moment, you are merely a shadow of a former existence.

Something so distant, like a lost vessel with no way to call for help.

At this moment, my heart closes the door—never to open to anguish
at your hands.

I think back to the possibilities and realities. I think my mind was
clouded, my heart was dull.

Each time of your return, I was setting myself up for this.

Your request is denied. Your request is selfish.

At this moment, I realize how unimportant I am to you, but how
important I am to me.

I matter, even if you don't think so.

Focused

Lindar was now forced to find something to fill her time. Even with TJ and basketball season, and Benjamin with all of his energy, she would always run into that time when they were sleep, not home, or simply not paying her any attention that Lindar would feel the void of Cajun. She had the skeleton of her book, and she had no idea what to do with it. She submerged herself into the Internet, looking for copyright and self-publishing information. As soon as the boys were out for the night, she was online, trying to figure it out. She was determined that if she did nothing else, she would have this book self-published just so that she could say that she did it.

Each day, Lindar read over the writings many times, thinking about all that she had been through. Some days, tears fell and, some days, she felt the strength to keep moving on. Oftentimes, it was TBN, The Word Network, a plethora of gospel artists and her Bible that pulled her through. In reference to her favorite Bible verse, Romans 8:28, she knew that this was all working together for her good. It didn't feel good, but she knew that what God was doing in her life was good.

Google became Lindar's best friend, taking her to sites to get the information she needed. She eventually stepped out on faith and had *Ghetto Chick* copyrighted. Once she completed that process, she felt like she was on her way. Every time she thought of Cajun, she pressed her way through by not calling him or texting him.

For self-publishers, there was so much good information for Lindar to read through. She knew that, aesthetically, she had to change her book. Night after night, she sat at the computer and changed the fonts. She removed images. Editing was an ongoing process, and she was constantly reading the edits—to the point that Benjamin knew *Run Tell That* almost by heart. Lindar cracked up every time she heard her three-year-old son belt out, "Who riddy used who? Run tell dat!"

❦

Finally, after months of research and finding a site online to upload to, Lindar released *Ghetto Chick* to the world. For her, it was just a self-proclamation fulfilled. She wasn't expecting much. That was all about to change. During this process, Lindar had learned to network. She was on Facebook and Twitter, and had started to increase traffic to her blog site. She had met other authors and listened to their advice about marketing and promotions. All of this information had been absorbed and Lindar had released an incredible book of writings of a broken heart, loneliness and her adoration for her children and God.

What Lindar was not prepared for was the success of the book or people's reaction to it. However, she knew she was created for such a time as this.

Unveiling

Upon receiving notice that people were purchasing her book and really reading their thoughts online, her friend Jen came up with the event idea that she was purposely avoiding.

"Why not have a book signing event?"

"I don't know."

"What?! You can't be serious. Come on. It'll be real simple to do," Jen encouraged. "We can have it at church. We can do some invites to friends, family and media. Put a table out with you and *Ghetto Chick* with some media print. Some light snacks and my mama's lemonade."

"Your mama's lemonade? Oh! That would have to go on the invite."

"Lindar, this would be good for you and your brand that you alone are building up. The book sells for what, five dollars? Even if we only sell ten or twenty, the event would be a success. You can even read some of your writings at the event."

"Me? Hit the mic? Check one, Check two? I'll think about it."

"Good! I'll start working on it."

"I said, I'll *think* about it."

"Okay. Then, I will work on it while you *think* about it."

Because of Jen's uber talent in communications, in a matter of days, she had *Ghetto Chick ~ The Initial Event* already planned. The location was set, the invitations were ready, and all Lindar had to do was take this leap of faith and make it happen. The problem was that Lindar still feared what others thought about her failed marriage to Tito and her unsuccessful relationship with Cajun. With that, she thought back to all of her failed relationships and how they didn't last. She thought about how each man she had loved had left her inclusive of her first love and the man that she would, later in life, go to the altar with. In her mind, there was no way that anyone would want to purchase her book or hear what she had to say.

❧

"So, everything is pretty much planned, I hear."

"Yes. Mia, Jen did an incredible job."

"I spoke with Jen and she said you don't seem excited about the event."

Sitting with Mia forced one to spill their heart. Lindar had no choice at this moment.

"I'm excited."

"Are you?"

"I thought Cajun and I would work out. In this moment, I feel like I should be sharing it with him."

"Who left?"

"What?"

"Lindar? Who left who? Even if it was bad, and things were not going well, if he loved you, he would have tried harder. He would have stayed. He left you."

"Just like everyone else."

"Lindar, you can't be serious. Really? You can't be."

"It's true. Any relationship that I ever had, from a teenager till now, they all left me. For whatever reason, I guess," Lindar confided.

"No. No. Stop. Lindar, this is bigger than Cajun and Tito. What you are saying is bigger than them. Yes, Cajun loved you, and Tito was your husband. But you've carried the hurt from years ago."

"Maybe..."

"There's no maybe. We've been friends since seventh grade. I know you. Girl, in order to find who God truly has for you, you have to release that hurt completely. He's moved on with his life. In a sense, you have, too. I think this is why you don't step out on your creativity because you've created this wall of fear that no one will like you or your writings," Mia said.

"Mia, sometimes I'd just rather stay in my home and do nothing.
I hate going out to social functions, period. I don't date. All I do is work and go to church."

"That's probably all you needed to do. But God had gifted you in so many areas. It's time you take your story of brokenness and bless another woman so that she'll know that she can make it through. The newness in you begins with this event. Mary, Jen and I know what's in you. Only you can bring it out."

"True. I'll call Jen and sound more excited."

"I hope so. We've changed the name of the event."

"To what?"

"Libations and Lemonade. Since we will be at church, we will keep the lemonade flowing."

"Oh! Wow! I like that. Libations and Lemonade ~ A Ghetto Chick Event."

"See! That's what I'm talking about. Now the event is on Saturday."

"Saturday? Today is Tuesday! What?" Lindar said shockingly.

"Girl, all I can say is get it together. Get it together. Please be prepared because Jen had created a media blitz. She doesn't do anything small," Mia said.

"What do you know that I don't?"

"Let me just say that you need to call Jen ASAP, and you will need a hair and nail appointment. Girl, call Sana!"

"Right! Anything else?"

"Yeah, your whole outfit needs to be new. She found funding to set this thing off. It's a dream come true for both of you."

Face to Face

So many unbelievable things were occurring for Lindar. She couldn't believe how many people were moved by her book. The book signing was packed with so many people from her family, friends and church. Even a couple authors from Facebook and Twitter came to Cincinnati to show their support for Lindar. That meant so much that she decided to throw a huge party. This party was to show her supporters how much she appreciated them. To get the word out, she went on the air on WROM FM 82.8 to speak with DJ T.

"Okay, Lindar. The buzz is out about the party."

"I know. I'm so overwhelmed by the love and support."

"Did you think *Ghetto Chick* would be so well received?"

"DJ T., I'm still in awe of everything."

"Yeah, we see. Kelly Rowland will be in the building. Sanaa Lathan! Latifah! Goodness girl, you shutting it down!"

"Honestly T., these are women who I've loved. They've shown it back to me by making an appearance at this event, and I really appreciate that. Now my girls from Cincy will be in the building, too. When Kelly sings "Like This," it's going to go completely crazy! That's my theme song right there!"

"Am I invited?"

"Boy, please! You already know! I have to let everyone know that when I met you at a book fair years ago, it was all love from the beginning and I haven't forgotten that."

"Let's take a break and come back with Lindar about her smash book and the over-the-top party tonight."

149

"WROM Rome 82.8 on the FM dial. This is DJ T. back with Lindar, local self-published sensation. Author of *Ghetto Chick*."

"Hello!"

"Next book, Sumthing Special."

"Alright now!"

"Off the chart party tonight."

"Get! Get! Get it!"

"Girl, you're off the chain. Phones are lighting up like crazy. First of all, how can you be reached?" DJ T. asked.

"Facebook, Twitter, LindarInsights.blogspot.com."

"Will you be doing any workshops locally?"

"Yes," Lindar replied.

"When?"

"I don't know." Lindar and DJ T. laughed at each other's silliness.

"I guess you wouldn't know, with the schedule you have."

"I would love to come back and teach a writing workshop. I've learned a lot over the years and I truly believe in paying it forward. There are so many great writers with great stories to tell."

"Seriously now, in both books, you wrote about personal pain. How are you now?"

"I'm good and in a good place. A really good place."

"T.J. Sr.?"

"I'm cordial. We share sons. I'm over the failed marriage and I've healed from him leaving us."

"Y'all kick it? He check ya' boy out on the court? Junior doing it big."

"Nope, he's never seen him play on a college court."

"You bitter?"

"Naw! I lounge in the parents VIP. I'm good.com."

"Okay, Ms. VIP!"

"Don't get it twisted. Shout out to my basketball moms. Now that's a real reality show. Let me get a payday loan to cover some of these AAU fees. Real talk."

"Girl, you a mess!"

"Moms of hoopers ain't full of drama. We trying to figure out how to stay at the Disney Resort and eating for a week with some 6'5," size 14 shoe-wearing man/child. All while covering the rent and mortgage back home. Hello! Oh, and don't let the cable be cut off when you get back home. That's just another headache."

"Sounds like a book."

"Already in the process."

"How do you find the time to do so much?"

"T., I wasted enough time on nonsense. God says my time is now. We all know time waits for no one."

"So, what's next?"

"Ghana," Lindar revealed.

"Ghana?"

"Yeah, I am working with a gospel artist who wants to record his next CD live from his hometown. We'll be there for three weeks."

"Wow! Right, to whom much is given…"

"Say that! Say that! So much more is required."

"Okay, you have to go. But I have to ask about Cajun."

"I've only seen him once since we broke up. He knew all of these things would happen for me. He told me years ago."

"Any feelings for him?"

"Nope."

"What's his real name?"

"Nope, won't tell. He knows who he is."

"If you saw him face to face, what would you say to him?"

"I'd share a smile and keep it moving."

"There you have it. Ms. Lindar from Cincy doing big things. Any last words to our listeners?"

"To everyone in Cincy who has supported me, my family and my projects, I just want to thank you for your love and support. I love y'all so much. To any woman out there dealing with brokenness, take your seeds somewhere else for them to grow. Love *you* more than you love *him*. This is Lindar of LindarInsights, signing out from WROM Rome 82.8 on your FM dial. See ya!"

Thank You

I want to thank my parents, James and Natalie McGlothin for raising up an intelligent and creative soul. To my brother and sister, James and Marlene, for years of support. James and Nae, I love you to life. Ryan aka Ry Ry Rizzle. I am so proud of you and you have played such an important role in this book and in my life. Chiiiillleee we've evolved. You have always had the ability to question me in a way that is both annoying and sensible. You truly make me see myself.

To Mommy's pumpkins, Alex and Tyler I stay crazy in awe with the both of you. Alex I know you will continue to bless others with your patience and knowledge about the sport of basketball. Your life is a blessing of both God's favor and healing powers. I love how you take everything in stride. The best is yet to come. At six months a nurse informed us that Tyler was a comedian. We see it now, for real. Everyone knows that you are going to do incredible things in life. Every rebound is yours.

To my girlfriends, Stephanie, Mischa, T'wanda, Alisa, Natasha, Destiny, Enjoli, Lauren, Quiera, Natalie, Curtrese, Peaches, Rasheeda and Lady Kisha thank you so much for your support over the years.

Noble, you are the bomb.com, my road dog and forever my BFF. Words can't express what you mean to me.

Greg you came in late in the game and asked the hard questions and forced me to come out of my shell and into the light. I thank you for all that you have done for me. There's a book in you. You are truly a renaissance man and a true gentleman. Adore!!

Pastor Mike Scruggs thank you for teaching me to think big. "My enough may not be your enough. Don't stop til you get enough" Light of the World Ministries has blessed our home and our lives. Keep doing incredible things. With this release, I'm getting out of the boat and I'm shooting my shot.

To all of the readers, thank you for picking up *Infused*. It's a testament of endurance and being transparent. Sometimes we end up in situations that are hurtful and embarrassing, but I believe the ability to share that pain allows others to see your transparency and know that they are not alone.

God has blessed me with a gift, and I share with you pieces of me. Right now, I'm in the waiting pattern. Just waiting on those things that God has for me. I finally realize exactly how special I am and that I deserve more than I have been allowing myself to obtain.

Connect with me on social media and on my websites.

www.lindarinsights.blogspot.com

www.lindarinsights.com

Twitter ~ @lindarinsights
Facebook ~ @lindarinsights
Instagram ~ @lindarinsightspublishing
Snapchat ~ @lindarinsights
Pinterest ~ @lindarinsights

To contact me for speaking engagements or to facilitate a writing or self-publishing workshop contact me at
lindarinsights@gmail.com

More Books By The Author

Ghetto Chick ©2009
#hespoilsme ©2016
Diligently ©2019
My Daily Gratitude Journal @2019

A man's gift makes room for him and brings him before great men.
Proverbs 18:16

Discover your gift! Let it make room for you!